Stumbling through Italy

Stumbling through Italy

Tales of Tuscany, Sicily, Sardinia, Apulia, Calabria and places in-between

Niall Allsop

ISBN 1-45384-978-5

ISBN-13 978-1-453849-78-1

Published by In Scritto *Italy in writing*
www.inscritto.com

Cover and book design by Niall Allsop – niallsop@mac.com

Main text set in Sabon
Additional notes and captions set in Frutiger
Cover and titles set in Broadsheet

For Ivano and Vittorio Capetti

Ma chi l'avrebbe mai detto ...!

Acknowledgements

I am indebted to the following for their part in getting this book into print:
Kay Bowen
Ivano Capetti
Vittorio Capetti
Rona Fineman

... and all the generous people we encountered on our Italian travels

Contents

It all began with an Indian

Kay and I have just witnessed a bizarre event.

It's summer 2006 in deepest Calabria, the toe of Italy.

Football's World Cup has just got under way and we are sitting enjoying a glass of cold white wine in the *piazza* of the small hilltop town of Siberene in the shadow of its imposing Norman castle. The fruit and veg man has just parked up his van and he too is having a lunchtime tipple.

Carlo, our host, ambles between tables talking to his customers mainly about the recent unsettled weather. The ever-present pigeons strut their stuff between the tables looking for scraps.

Suddenly, from the fruit and veg man's table there is a flurry of fingers and feathers, a squeal of delight, Carlo and a few others laugh and Kay and I look at each other in amazement … did we really see what we think we saw?

The fruit and veg man gets up from his table and displays his prize for all to see. He is holding a flapping pigeon by the feet. Without being told, Kay and I both know the next bit. The fruit and veg man was not showing off his dexterity, nor was he serving a civic function by getting rid of the pigeons … he was catching dinner, if not for himself then for a friend, perhaps even a customer.

He headed for his van with his prize, dispatched it out of sight of his curious public and returned to his table ... for fruit and veg man, now read fruit, veg and pigeon man.

Now there's not a lot of meat on a pigeon so, I suppose, what happened next was sort of inevitable. Our pigeon fancier asked Carlo to replenish his dish of peanuts and with fresh supplies set about fooling another hapless bird into lowering his or her guard and within a couple of minutes there's a second pigeon for the pot ... and two fewer pigeons around the square.

My first reaction is to write to our local rag, the *Bath Chronicle,* and suggest that the city hire this guy right away and in so doing solve both the local pigeon (and seagull) problem *and* introduce the good people of Bath to two new delicacies, pigeon pie and stuffed seagull.

Kay doesn't think it would go down too well in England.

I agree but nevertheless I think I should still write to the *Bath Chronicle*. I did. And the letter was published. I believe the Council continue to consider the matter.

Being there, in that square, on that day and watching the normalities of life in what seemed a typical hilltop town caused me to reflect on all the other times we had been to Italy in recent years. Our first visit was in September 1999, since when we have returned at least twice a year, mainly to the deep south as well as Sardinia and Sicily. Over that time we had read many travelogues about the places we had been (and some places we hadn't been) but these were all written by people based in Italy or with family there. And, of course, the writers usually spoke fluent Italian.

What about people like us? We had made inroads into the language but always felt inadequate. We didn't live there, we didn't have family there, we just loved the place. Yet, despite the difficulties of communication, every time we went to Italy we got drawn into people's lives, we had adventures and encounters that 'normal' people didn't seem to have on holiday. Almost innocently we absorbed the Italian way (whatever that is or was), we made friends; when we arrived we were just another two tourists and often when we left we were *famiglia*.

That day made me realise that, though our experiences in Italy may or may not be unique, they definitely deviate from the norm and, as such, are worthy of record.

We *do* do something different when we're there but we're not sure what it is … perhaps seeing it unfold on the page will explain all. Perhaps some canny reader can work it out.

*

It all began with an Indian meal. We left the restaurant and crossed the road to window-shop the Oxfam*.

This was affluent Bath where the charity shops all seemed to be a cut above the rest. Of course, we never actually bought anything but enjoyed speculating whether those glasses or that hat or this book were bargains or not. Just along from the shop was one of those A-frames advertising an Italian restaurant, Capetti's. We both spotted it at the same time and there and then decided that next time we ate out we'd try Bath's new Italian restaurant.

We did, but we were wrong. This 'new' Italian had been here, on this very spot, for over eleven years. We'd simply missed it, never noticed it before, never even heard anyone mention it.

But this underground haphazard shrine to all things Italian,

*For non-UK readers, Oxfam is a renowned international Oxford-based aid organisation; to help fund its work, Oxfam has many so-called charity shops throughout the UK which sell second-hand clothes and books and other nicknacks, usually donated by the public.

especially Italian football and Ferrari cars, and to pre-Russian Chelsea* soon became our regular place to eat out and it wasn't long before we were on first name terms with Vittorio, 'Vic', the waiter and his younger brother, the chef, Ivano.

We were introduced to their late father through the photo on the wall and the fascinating story of how he had left his native Scansano in Tuscany and come to Bath after the Second World War looking for work as a miner. Here he met and married a fellow countrywoman and settled down to a life in the Somerset coalfields until, that is, he had the bright idea of opening an Italian delicatessen in Bath which, in turn, brought Vittorio and Ivano into the catering business. Compelling though that story was, it was essentially an English story ... just as intriguing was the supposed origin of the family name, the Capetti name.

It seems that Capetti is not a common Italian family name; indeed, apart from close family, it appears to be almost non-existent elsewhere in the country and Italian communities world-wide. The story is that grandfather Capetti was an abandoned orphan who was brought up nameless in a nunnery**. When the time came for him to leave the fold, he needed a family name and so the nuns, Caterina, Angelina,

---

*Non-UK readers should also note that Chelsea is a London-based football (soccer) club which, since 2003, has been Russian-owned.

**From mediæval times women in Italy and other European countries often took advantage of the so-called 'wheel' to secure a better life for newborn infants that they felt unable to keep. The wheel, usually set into a convent wall, was a wooden turntable with a number of separate compartments or boxes where people could leave food and other contributions for the convent; all the nuns had to do was rotate the wheel from inside the wall. Any infant placed in the 'wheel' would likewise find itself inside the convent where it would be brought up. Some Italians with the family name Esposito can trace their origins back to this practice as it was often a name given to orphans 'exposed' in this way.
Eventually the practice fell into disrepute though in some larger cities it appears to have been re-introduced in a more sanitised, 21st century way with the so-called 'drop-off windows'.

Paola, Elena, Tazia, Teresa and Isabella put their heads together and, well ... I'm sure you've worked it out.

When the Capetti brothers first told me this story, my smut-button kicked in and I couldn't resist suggesting that they were really lucky that the nuns hadn't been called Francesca, Ursula, Camilla, Katerina, Emelia and Donetta which, thank goodness, they both thought was very funny.

Now this, it seemed to me, was an Italian story. Even without my contribution, there was a sort of irreverence about it. It didn't matter whether it was true or not, it felt intrinsically Italian ... and I had never even been there.

For the previous five years Kay and I had holidayed mainly in Portugal but the time was right for a change and so it was that, early one evening, we descended into Capetti's with an idea and a map. We wanted to eat, spread the map out on the table and plan our next jaunt ... to northern Spain!

I'm not really quite sure why we chose Spain, let alone northern Spain, but all thoughts of touring the Basque country were soon dispelled when Vic took one look at our intended destination, rolled his eyes in disgust, unhooked a lopsided map of Italy from the wall and plonked it on the table. His jabbing finger said, 'This is where you should go'.

And we did.

Six weeks later we took off from London Gatwick on an Alitalia flight to Pisa where we picked up a car and headed east towards Arezzo and the eastern extremity of Tuscany (Toscana).

A note on names, maps and language

In some cases I have changed people's names. Usually there is an obvious reason for this, though in a few cases I had forgotten the name. That said, most of people herein are exactly who I say they are. I have also changed the name of one town and two places where we stayed; again there are particular reasons for having done so.

Most of the place names mentioned in the text are included on the accompanying maps which are normally on the first or second page of each chapter that introduces a new location. These are to varying scales depending on the area they cover but each includes a rough indication of the distances involved.

I have introduced Italian words and phrases which either have an obvious meaning (*anniversario di matrimonio*) or are the sorts of words and phrases (*dov'è Bruno?* – where is Bruno? or *vicolo* – alleyway) that I wish I'd known when I first went to Italy. With regard to town names I sometimes use the Italian, sometimes the English, though not entirely in a haphazard way – where they are different I start with the English and introduce the Italian.

Finally, I have used international English throughout as opposed to American English: autumn for fall; football for soccer, colour for color; centre for center; realise for realize ... and so on. Most readers will be conversant with the language of both cultures and can make the switch; the most difficult cultural characteristic to overcome is the realisation that American football and football (soccer) in the rest of the world are two different games.

Monterchi and the VM with child

Our preparation had been faultless. Courtesy of *The Guardian*'s small ads, we were going to stay near the village of Monterchi in an old *casa colonica* (farmhouse) that had been restored and renovated by a London couple who planned to live there eventually. In the meantime, while the work continued on the top floor, the rest was available to rent. The transaction had been completed by post and just before we left we received the key (not a Yale, you understand, but a proper key, the sort you might imagine hanging from a monk's belt) and the directions from Pisa to Arezzo and then on to Monterchi itself.

Our flight was on schedule and so we reckoned on arriving at the house around ten in the evening. Everything went according to plan: we headed east from Pisa, circumnavigated Florence (Firenze) successfully and survived the wrong turn that we were told takes you straight into the red-light district, (I remember thinking at the time that it seemed strange that a city such as Florence would even have a red-light district), went through Arezzo and on towards Monterchi. When we reached the town it was already dark but we had our detailed directions, although these omitted to mention that our arrival might possibly coincide with the local Polenta Festival.

EMILIA-ROMAGNA

Adriatic Sea

Rimini

SAN MARINO

MARCHE

Pisa

Florence

Chianti region

San Gimignano

Arezzo

MONTERCHI

Siena

Lake Trasimeno

TUSCANY

Perugia

Elba

UMBRIA

Tyrrhenian Sea

LAZIO

Pisa to Florence · 95km

18

Naïve we undoubtedly were. I mean, now we know that almost every weekend, in every small town in Italy there is a *festa*, a festival, an excuse for a party. As I write, it's the day after Italy's 2006 World Cup victory and they'll probably even have a party for that! Any excuse whatsoever ... I've even seen posters encouraging the faithful to participate in a town's *Trippa Festa*, Tripe Festival. No thanks, I thought.

I remain uncertain as to what a Polenta Festival is or does but that night it seemed to lure hundreds of people to this small hilltop town and the resulting traffic chaos bordered on anarchy. Now that I've got a few years' experience of driving in Italy behind me, I would be quite confident about negotiating two festivals on the same night in Monterchi or even Naples – I would simply drive like an Italian, I would just ignore everybody and everything, press on regardless, if necessary go up or down a few one-way streets and I'd be confident that we'd come out the other end unscathed and nearer our destination.

But this was our first brush with the Italian psyche so we played it by the rules (albeit English rules) and stopped to ask a man in uniform (possibly a policeman but in Italy not necessarily so as we were to discover) to help us through the chaos and on to our holiday home.

When I say 'ask' of course our Italian was virtually non-existent. We were armed with the excellent BBC phrasebook and a piece of paper with the address but between us we had three pairs of hands. It was the hands that saw us through and on our way out of Monterchi and back into the countryside with a rough idea of where we were going. Beyond the town and its on-going Polenta party, we turned right off the main road and up yet another winding hill towards the hamlet of Fonaco. The directions seemed clear enough and we thought that at last the end was in sight ... except, of course, that it was dark, very dark.

Monterchi

Following a brief difference of opinion, I conceded and we turned left off the road and approached the silhouette of a house, a house with an ageing Renault 4 lurking in the bushes. The barking of a distant dog broke the silence ... a closer, responding bark added to our twitchiness. Were there any wolves in Tuscany, I wondered, making a mental note to Google wolves and Tuscany when I got back home ... if I got back home.

Of course this was the house, it fitted the description, well, more or less, and we were bloody tired and it would do! I still wasn't sure but felt that, if all else failed, at least we could eliminate this from the list. We crept forward to the door, Kay clutching the key in a nervous hand. She tried it in the lock, this way and that way ... and it didn't work. The words 'I told you so' were on the tip of my tongue but I thought better of it and suggested that we read the directions again just in case WE had make a mistake.

Up and down and round that road we went until, weary and disorientated, we turned off to the left and parked outside what proved to be our goal, the beautiful Casa Fonaca, complete with *il pipistrello* (bat). Of course at the time, we didn't know it was beautiful but, after a good night's sleep, our first in Italy, we were ready to explore and take in our environs.

We had hit the jackpot. The setting was glorious with the hills of Umbria on the one side and the gentler slopes of Tuscany rolling down to Monterchi on the other, the perfect place to wind down and relax.

When we retraced our steps to Monterchi the next day, in daylight, we wound down the hillside past fields of sunflowers (sadly not in flower) and there, a few kilometres away down in the valley, was a fortress-topped hill overseeing a scattering of houses, a multi-coloured island in a verdant sea. It was shimmering and inviting in the early morning haze, light years it seemed from the chaos of the night before and the pleasures of the Polenta. We looked forward to exploring this 'island' of Monterchi and finding somewhere to eat later in the day.

Within the town's walls (in one case literally) there were two restaurants, one basically for locals and the other, a little more up-market, geared more to visitors. Naturally we plumped for the former, not once but every night, and normally we were the only non-Italians there.

The *Vecchia Osteria* (the old inn), was run by a hard-working husband-and-wife team, Enzo and Adrianna, who had a simple menu system – for the *primo piatto* (the first, usually pasta, course) there was a choice from any of six sauces and any six pastas, 36 meals in total, all the same price; each night there was also a list of about half a dozen meat courses, the *secundo piatto*, to choose from. Pretty simple and bloody good. Each night we ate and drank, watched the television and chatted with the locals ... actually one local in particular (let's call him Bruno) who, like us, was a regular.

When I say 'chatted' Bruno did most of the chatting and we did most of the grunting, nodding and '*Si*'-ing. Each evening the television news clearly got him worked up and he would share his views about this and that and naturally we agreed with everything he said ... we knew that our trusty BBC phrasebook was next to useless in this situation. What we didn't realise at the time was that, in the complex world of Italian politics, that particular week was building up to a climax that was to divide the nation ... and our eating companion was getting pretty worked up about one side of the argument. It was not until a couple of years later that I managed to fit together the pieces of this particular jigsaw.

I was reading Peter Robb's brilliant *Midnight in Sicily* the conclusion of which revisited the day the verdict was delivered after the trial of the Italian politician and seven-times Prime Minister, Giulio Andreotti. On 24 September 1999 Andreotti was cleared of ordering the murder of investigative journalist Mino Pecorelli in 1974. Implicit in the charges was the allegation that Andreotti had mafia connections. When I read this, the penny dropped and I realised that we had been there, we were actually sitting in *Vecchia Osteria* when the verdict came through on the television news.

So this explained why our friend Bruno, clearly an Andreotti sympathiser, was ecstatic. He thumped the table and rattled on excitedly both verbally and manually. Of course we agreed with every last detail of his argument ... though, having read and re-read Peter Robb's book, I'm now not so sure.

While all this was going on we were desperately trying to change the subject and get everyone to focus on a far more important event ... today was our *anniversario di matrimonio*. At last Enzo got the message and we were toasted by all and sundry and, better still, none of the additional *liquori* found their way onto *il conto*, the bill. It was to be a bad week for Enzo as the next evening he had to contend with yet another financial setback ... it was *il mio compleanno,* my birthday! Coincidentally, the following March, on Kay's birthday, we were once again sitting in the *Vecchia Osteria* drinking the profits.

All road signs to Monterchi are accompanied by another sign pointing the way to the town's only real claim to fame, the *Madonna del Parto*, a 15th century fresco depicting the pregnant Virgin Mary. Apparently there are only two such early depictions of the VM with child and the fresco in Monterchi is the only one in Italy. Now, I'm not into icons of any kind, whether it be Madonna or *the* Madonna, and so we never did pop into the small museum to view the fresco.

Apparently expectant mothers can go in and compare bumps for free though, as I understand it, there are no guarantees that the actual birth might have global implications. For the miserly unpregnant, reproductions of the fresco were not exactly uncommon in and around the town; there was even one in Casa Fonaco, company for *il pipistrello*.

We split our time between relaxing in the garden, wandering round Monterchi's narrow streets absorbing every alleyway, every arch, every ageing door and worn step and, of course, exploring as much of Tuscany and Umbria as we could reasonably fit in. We drove as far as Siena and the Chianti region to the west and south to Perugia, and Lago Trasimeno. At Arezzo we caught the super-fast train to Rome, just for the day – to date our sole visit to the capital, though we have flown there many times.

Looking back I suppose we were acclimatising ourselves with Italy: we were sussing it out, learning the wrinkles, observing the rituals and wondering whether it was worth a second visit. Apart from Siena, we were disappointed in most of the touristy places; apart from Monterchi most of the Tuscan hill towns were the same and would never make it into any future itinerary. One particularly famous one, San Gimignano, was a huge disappointment and, following our late afternoon visit, we beat a hasty retreat and drove furiously due east to our own little hill-top town that we hoped would never make it onto any tourist trail ... apart from the few VM-with-child-watchers.

I've already mentioned that we were used to holidaying in Portugal; we had even toyed with the idea of buying a property (more of a ruin actually) in southern Portugal but were put off by the shenanigans of the ex-pat network there. Of course it's not uncommon for groups of foreigners to come together but it sort of defeated the object if it meant that you never really got to learn the language or socialise with the indigenous population. When we were contemplating the idea ourselves, we felt we could do it differently and rise above it all ... perhaps that was wishful thinking, but we'll never know.

In Tuscany we experienced none of this. No doubt there were English enclaves somewhere but, despite Tuscany's reputation for seducing the unsuspecting foreigner – usually British, French or American – and forcing them to write books about their experiences in this or that hilltop town, restoring this or that farm, we never were aware of an émigré network. And this despite having read some of the books (*Under the Tuscan Sun* and *The Hills of Tuscany*) and visited all the towns mentioned therein in search of these enslaved scribblers. It's interesting that, at the time of writing, the Amazon website throws up 15,890 books on Tuscany, more than Italy's three most southerly provinces, Puglia, Basilicata and Calabria, put together.

But there were other aspects of Italian life that intrigued and sometimes foxed us.

When we first drove through Monterchi en route to Casa Fonaco and *il pipistrello,* I was a driving-in-Italy virgin but now I felt like Tom Hanks in the film *Cast Away* when, having knocked out his own tooth with an ice-skate, he became a new, almost superhuman, person. It didn't take long to assimilate the rules – it seemed simple enough, there were no rules – and I could feel my new improved powers envelop me. I never did get the one that allowed me to see round bends but at the end of eleven days driving I had become almost native (of course several years of driving in Portugal may have contributed). That said, I only got the one parking ticket so maybe I still had a few things to learn!

The more I drive there, the more I begin to realise that my first impressions may have been misleading ... but more of that later.

Italy has historical heritage in abundance. Even the smallest of small towns will boast something of historical interest. We soon discovered that all we had to do was follow the signs for the *centro storico*, which invariably took us up to or past something of note ... the down side being that, as likely as not, we would end up in the narrowest of one-way *vicoli* (alleyways) with no obvious means of escape. On more than one occasion the *vicolo* came to an abrupt end at the top edge of a flight of descending steps ... and on one occasion I thought, bugger it, I'll drive down these! I'd seen it done in *The Italian Job* so it must have been okay.

With so much of it about, I suppose it's not surprising that Italians have their own peculiar slant on making the past accessible. On that first trip a couple of places caused us to wonder just exactly what was going on, indeed if *anything* was going on.

I've already mentioned the many *Madonna del Parto* signs in and around Monterchi and yet in Pisa it took us ages to locate the famous leaning tower precisely because, at the time, there *weren't* any signs. We stopped locals and asked for directions and, yes, our Italian left a lot to be desired, but it wasn't that bad: some didn't know (or understand?) while others gave conflicting directions. No matter, we eventually stumbled upon it. You see, we were looking for the wrong place ... we should have been looking for the Piazza del Duomo, the square by the cathedral where the tower stood. We were looking *in* the wrong place too for, it being a tower, we expected to see it on the skyline; we didn't realise that, in the towering stakes, Pisa's effort was more on the stumpy side and was in fact dwarfed by most of the surrounding buildings.

On the other hand, Perugia, the capital of Umbria, embraces its past in quite a different way. Here what you see is not all you get. The car parks are spaced round the virtually traffic-free city to which they are linked by a series of escalators but the one from the Piazza Partigiani is special in that it runs through the underground mediæval city to the main square, Piazza Italia. Now, this being Italy, there did not seem to be anything incongruous in this mix of modern escalators and mediæval streets and shops ... indeed to use these shops for exhibitions and cultural events seemed only the next logical step.

One minute you're in a car park, next your heading underground, then you're walking along a well-lit mediæval street, complete with street names and, before you emerge back into the bright sunlight of the Piazza Italia and today's Perugia, you might want to stop off at one of the mediæval shops to buy a guitar. Yes, when we were there, most of the shops were playing host to various aspects of the music industry; the mediæval experience was for the tourists and the practical use of the space was for locals and tourists alike. It's a bit like Stonehenge hosting a garden furniture extravaganza and stringing up a hammock between a couple of the stones!

Over the years we've started to come to terms with this off-the-wall view of the past and its artefacts but this first experience left us a little confused – we couldn't work out what, if anything, the Pisa and the Perugia experiences had in common? It took many more visits to Italy for some sort of explanation to evolve, the penny was a long time in the dropping ...

It's really quite simple (at least I think it is). The Italians are cool about the past, it is no big deal, it's all around them, it's haphazard in an orderly sort of way, sometimes orderly in a haphazard sort of way ... it's there to be both appreciated and functional, not there to be mollycoddled, not there as some sort of constipated, explicit experience. It is, above all else, a normal part of the present.

One other aspect of our first Italian experience outwitted us day after day and even on into our next visit. Nowadays it's no problem, we have been the victors, no more will we fall for the scourge of the *siesta*.

It so happens that both Kay and I enjoy a bit of retail therapy; Italy is, after all, a good place to buy the likes of clothes, shoes and leather. But, picture the scenario: up in the morning, have a lazy breakfast out in the sun, nip into Monterchi for a walk and a coffee, possibly even *una pasta* (not pasta but the wonderful Italian pastries bought in a *pasticceria*) before setting off on a leisurely drive to have a look at, say, Arezzo. Nothing could be simpler, except that when we got to Arezzo or wherever, everything (except cafés, bars and restaurants) was closing down for four hours! To make matters worse, once the shops shut, they are often shuttered too so sometimes it's impossible to tell which buildings are indeed shops which puts the kibosh on window-shopping. Even local supermarkets close.

Day after day we did the same thing, we'd arrive in a town, park up and, if we were lucky, have half an hour before the shutters came down – scarcely time to try on a baseball cap. On the plus side, we couldn't buy much and the parking was always free for the duration of the *siesta*!

Eventually we learnt to beat the system by leaving for longer jaunts to towns and cities early in the morning and returning to base for a quiet afternoon after they shut up shop; then, if we wanted another trip out, we'd make sure we got there between five and six in the evening when the streets were coming back to life. It seems simple enough but for us northern Europeans it's not a natural process and there were to be times in the future when we'd arrive somewhere and both look at each other with that we've-done-it-again look!

So, having found the leaning tower of Pisa and acquired our first parking ticket on the same day, we headed for the airport and home, our heads buzzing with the wonders of this new-found country.

It was unspoken, but we both knew that we'd definitely be back. More than anywhere else we'd visited we knew that somehow we belonged here ... which makes it even more reprehensible that we didn't make a bigger effort to learn the language.

Back in Bath we relived the holiday with the Capetti brothers and anyone else who would listen. I'm sure we bored the pants off people but the experience had left its mark ... our only regret was that we never did find that winding row of *cipressi* (cypress trees) that invariably features on the front cover of books about all things Tuscan.

*

Six months later we returned to Monterchi.

This time we took advantage of a cheap, late-in-the-day Ryanair flight to the east-coast resort of Rimini where we stayed the night. Next morning, before we set off across and through the mountains of Le Marche en route to Monterchi, we made a slight detour to put my mind at rest.

When I was a child, and temporarily into stamp-collecting, I became interested in a place called San Marino through its penchant for *triangular* stamps. The only other information about San Marino that had registered since was that it was one of the world's smallest countries, was located within Italy and hosted a Formula One Grand Prix. With Rimini almost next door, it seemed impertinent not to call in and take a look.

La Repubblica di San Marino sits at the top of a hill, fifteen kilometres from the coast, and its main preoccupation seemed to be with being a tax haven. The 'outlets' alongside the winding road up to the top did their best to beseech us to pull over and buy something at a bargain price. We resisted, pressed onwards and upwards and parked up by the towers at the summit.

Despite the feeling that we had just stepped into a very sophisticated, olde-worlde marketplace, San Marino was an agreeable mix of the commercial and the historical. We spent time wandering round both, our only concession to the former being an enormous Ferrari banner we bought for the Capetti brothers before we visited one of the towers and were rewarded with the most spectacular views in all directions and in particular the shimmering coast of the Adriatic.

I learnt three things that morning: San Marino is the world's smallest republic, the San Marino Grand Prix is *not* held in San Marino but at Imola some ninety kilometres north-west and, despite being well-known for its stamps, San Marino no longer issues the ones with three sides – such frivolities were just for the 1950s.

When we arrived back at Casa Fonaco that afternoon it was still daylight, there was no traffic chaos to negotiate, no Polenta Festival and no sign of *il pipistrello*. It was late March and, unlike England, spring was in the air; it wasn't as hot as it had been in September, particularly at night, but it was warm enough.

The welcome from Enzo and Adrianna was most unexpected, not only did it include the traditional Italian double kiss but there were also a few glasses of *grappa* (for me) and *limoncello* (for Kay) that appeared on the table but not on the bill. Once again we ate there every night, but this time without the excitable Bruno; sadly our Italian was not good enough to ask what had happened to him, even though it would have been simple to do so: *dov'è Bruno?* would have done the trick.

We struggled again with the *siesta* and somehow managed once more to turn up in a town that was just about to shut up shop. But not so on the day we went to Florence when we made a point of setting off early in the morning to get there around ten o'clock.

Everyone, it seemed, raved about Firenze so our curiosity got the better of us even though it had been our experience that the more we heard, 'You must go there, it's amazing', the more likely we were to be disappointed. I don't think this is a deliberate reaction, it's just that, even in the largest cities, we have a tendency to gravitate towards people rather than buildings and artefacts. We do not instinctively home in on the nearest church or cathedral when we visit a town ... we're more likely to head for the bar or café with the oldest men sitting outside, one of whom might well drag us off, kicking and screaming, to the nearest church on the mistaken assumption that that's why we're there.

It goes without saying that Firenze is a beautiful city, its golden stone and red roofs eclipsed by the grandeur of its more spectacular edifices. But my guess is that dawn is probably the best time to see it, and only then if you don't share your intent with any other human. At all other times its streets, squares and courtyards are teeming with traffic and tourists and that's how we found it.

At one point we thought we'd break with tradition and pop in to the Galleria dell'Accademia and pay our respects to Michelangelo's *David* but the length of the queue and slowness of its progress knocked that idea on the head. I mean, what's the point of being somewhere like Firenze and staring at someone else's backside for an hour and a half? In any case, we knew what this guy David looked like … overlarge head, overlong arms sporting large, out-of-proportion hands … size might not be everything but there's no excuse for screwing up the proportions!

So, instead, we headed for the Ponte Vecchia (Old Bridge), famous not only for its external architecture but also because it supports a corridor of shops, mostly jewellers and goldsmiths, one of only two such bridges in Europe … the other one, of course, is in Bath! We compared and contrasted and reckoned it was a draw: in the antiquity stakes the Ponte Vecchia won hands down, in terms of setting, the beautiful horseshoe weir downstream of Bath's Pulteney Bridge redressed the balance.

On our way back to Monterchi, we felt that we'd 'done' Firenze, but perhaps not done it justice; the *Vecchia Osteria* beckoned and that's where our tired, touristed-out bodies desperately wanted to be. That evening we would say farewell to Enzo and Adrianna and, back at Casa Fonaco, as we entered the downstairs hallway, we'd metaphorically doff a cap to our constant companion there, *il pipistrello*.

When we left Monterchi for the second time, we weren't sure whether we'd return or not; on the other hand neither were we sure where else we might go. Only one thing was certain, Italy hadn't seen the last of us.

Sex and socks in Sicily

A couple of times a year Kay meets up with three of her old college chums for a girls' weekend away. The gathering in late June was to be in London and she decided to extend the break by a couple of days and travel across on the Wednesday.

As I didn't qualify for an invite, I naturally headed straight for the Ryanair website and started to hunt for cheap flights to Italy. It was already Wednesday so the earliest I could fly out was the Thursday, back on the Monday. At the time I had no destination in mind but eventually landed a bargain to a place called Lamezia Terme in southern Calabria. I had no idea where that was or what was there but what I did spot was that it was fairly close to the tip of Italy's toe and therefore only a stone's throw from Sicily.

Sicily is one of those places that conjures up all sorts of intriguing images, invariably linked to men in dark glasses, darker suits and the darkest of intent. Movies such as the *Godfather* trilogy and television's tongue-in-cheek *Sopranos* series have ensured that the reputation of *La Cosa Nostra* (our thing), the mafia, is global. Obviously I wasn't immune to these preconceptions but, being of rational mind, I guessed they were only part of the truth and, besides, there was no way I was going to be that close to this fascinating island and

Tyrrhenian Sea

Aeolian Islands

Villa San Giovanni

Messina

Reggio di Calabria

SICILY

Mount Etna

Taormina

Enna

Catania

Villa Romana di Casale

Ionian Sea

SIRACUSA

Messina to Catania · 95km

not take a peek. The only other thing I knew about Sicily was that it was home to the spectacular Mount Etna, an active volcano that would still be around long after the mafia had gone.

Before setting off for Stansted Airport I had time to book a car at Lamezia but didn't get the chance to arrange anywhere to stay – bed that night was to be a surprise. And, yes, it turned out to be exactly that!

Travelling alone has its benefits, particularly when you fly with a budget airline that doesn't allocate seats, an economy that clearly puts a pressure on couples or families to find seats together. The lack of such pressure can be strangely liberating, even calming and the fact that I had no specific destination in mind for that evening didn't seem to matter.

The plane departed a little late and as soon as we were off the ground I unfolded my map of Sicily – this was all the airport bookshop had on the island but, if nothing else, it served a purpose in that it helped initiate conversation with my sole companion in the window seat.

"Heading for Sicily, then?" he said perceptively.

"I hope so ... depends on how easy it is to get across" I replied.

"Shouldn't be a problem, there's plenty of ferries from Reggio and Villa San Giovanni, it only takes about half an hour."

"You going to Sicily too?" I enquired.

"I'm hoping to but I'm stopping off to stay with a friend in Reggio for a couple of weeks first; I'll be in Italy for a month or so."

The ice broken, we went through the formalities of introductions, how we each made a living, where we lived, marital status ... the usual sorts of things that seem to matter when you first meet someone. Jack, a London-based architect, was gay. He didn't mention the latter but, having several gay friends, I just knew.

We talked mainly about travelling, finding cheap flights on the internet (we played a round of the inevitable lets-see-who's-found-the-cheapest-flight game – I won) and, as we both worked for ourselves from home, about our respective jobs.

As the flight progressed, our chit-chat was increasingly punctuated by Jack looking at his watch and the more he did so, the more agitated he seemed to become. When we eventually landed he explained that he had just missed his train to Reggio and that he wasn't sure if there was another that night.

Step forward Sir Galahad.

I had told Jack I'd be collecting a car at the airport and so, though I hadn't planned specifically to head for Reggio that evening, I was happy to do so and offered him a lift. I knew it was the sort of place where I'd easily find a hotel for the night.

Jack accepted my offer and, as we left the airport, made a call to his friend Paulo, a university lecturer in Reggio, to explain the change of plan – he'd now be arriving by car and that there'd be an extra mouth to feed and a bed to make ready. My accommodation in Reggio di Calabria had been sorted ... Kay's not going to believe this, I thought.

The welcome from Paulo and his friend Octavia was effusive, effusive and genuine; they were both delighted to see their friend from England and extended their welcome to me, his last-minute, straight companion and chauffeur.

I'd been in this position before. For some reason gay men often think that I might be gay or, more likely, they pick up that I am at ease with their sexual orientation. I have ways of telling them I'm straight and that's fine too so, all round, it's no problem, we all play by the same rules.

We ate and drank well, exceptionally well, though for much of the time my over-active mind was trying to work out the relationships between all these people. Jack and Paulo were clearly 'warm brothers', of that I was certain; Octavia was married and was on holiday from Milan to where she was returning the following day ... but there seemed more to her relationship with Paulo than met the eye. It was all too fascinating, not to mention speculative.

I was having a great time and not at all phased when Agnella arrived to say farewell to Octavia ... I was beginning to get the picture, albeit one that didn't fit in with my original alcohol-induced assessment.

The laughing and the drinking continued as the clock swept past two in the morning and we decided to call it a day ... Friday to be precise. But before we all hit the sack, it was agreed that after breakfast I would follow Paulo down to the ferry and that he'd see me on my way across to Messina in Sicily.

Breakfast came and went for five weary bodies – yet another culinary delight made all the more glorious by my first glimpse of Sicily, basking in the mid-morning sun in a limpid green sea. I was impatient to be out there, I just wanted to get the 'goodbyes' over with and get down to the ferry but this was Italy and I went along with the slower pace until Paulo was ready.

As he cranked up his scooter, his *motorino*, he gave me his number and insisted that I call him from Messina on my way back so that we all could have lunch together.

By the time the ferry cast off I felt I could almost touch Sicily; I recalled Paulo's story about the 1908 earthquake and could see how it was that most of both Messina and Reggio had been destroyed; Messina came off worse and here alone it was estimated that some 80,000 people, around two-thirds of the population, had died. Half-way over, a mere fifteen minutes into the crossing, I could clearly make out the tall concrete stilts of the *autostrada* running along behind the town and knew that it wouldn't be long before I was up there and heading south towards Etna.

My calculations hadn't allowed for the idiosyncrasies of Messina's late morning traffic and I was one weary, even perplexed, driver by the time I was clear of the town. It was my own fault, I had completely forgotten to have the injection that reprogrammed me for driving in Italy.

About an hour later I caught my first glimpse of the awesome Etna and left the *autostrada* to wind my way up towards the summit past an exhilarating mix of lush vegetation, black lava and spectacular views round every bend and in all directions.

What an experience. What an amazing experience marred only by a poor choice of footwear. I was wearing sandals and, as everyone knows, it's not cool to wear socks with sandals so, ever the slave to fashion, I didn't.

Big mistake. Big, big mistake.

At the time Etna's summit was covered in a very fine, cinder-like ash and it got everywhere ... in my case, the 'everywhere' I didn't want it to get was between my feet and my sandals. When it did (which was most of the time) it was like walking on broken glass. I loved and hated every minute of it: I loved being there in a place that had both raw beauty and such lethal potential at the same time; I hated having to stop every few minutes to sort out my feet and as a result missing so much of the guide's patter and his occasional statistics ... not that I would have understood a lot but I wanted to be part of it and not constantly standing on one leg like some sort of incontinent dog.

By the time I returned to the car, the pain had almost worn off – never was a pair of socks so welcome. I sat there and looked back up at where I'd just been and wished that I could have shared this experience with Kay. I knew I been somewhere very special, somewhere totally unique, almost primeval, and I knew she would have wanted to have been there too.

But first, back to reality and the minor problem of where I was going to sleep that night. I looked around the car park in case there were any waifs and strays that might want a lift somewhere and throw in accommodation in part-payment. I drew a blank with that and decided to opt for a more traditional route, a hotel. But where?

Paulo had posed that question earlier and rattled off a few place names accompanied by various grimaces that were probably designed to give me a clue as to *his* preferred destination. The one that stuck in my mind was Siracusa, Syracuse. It was a name that I recalled from somewhere but couldn't quite put my finger on where, when or why. I had also noticed the name on some of the road signs and, according to my trusty map, it was on the coast and not too far away. Now, if I'd had a guide book I might have saved myself a bit of time ...

A little over three hours later I was heading out of Siracusa disappointed, weary and bedless when suddenly I spotted three in a row ... hotels that is. I'd already spent a fruitless hour in the town centre and the only hotel I came up with was definitely not in my financial bracket. I wandered round aimlessly in ever-decreasing circles, getting more and more frustrated, and having come to the conclusion that Siracusa was a dump, returned to the car and decided to give the sprawling Catania the benefit of my patronage. If my route out of town hadn't been along this particular one-way street,

I would simply have got so much wrong and my life would have been the poorer for it.

The Hotel Archimede was not The Ritz nor was it the pits; it was cheap, cheerful and clean and I was tired and hungry; I booked in for two nights. I'd give this Siracusa place one last chance, I thought.

I washed my feet (they deserved it) and lay on the bed and marvelled that it was still less than twenty-four hours since I left Stansted. In my mind's eye I kept returning to Etna and as I did so the pain of getting there receded. I thought about how I could convey this experience to Kay, particularly as I'd come all this way without my camera. It was then that I realised I'd have to show her in person very soon ... very, very soon ... within the next fortnight or so anyway.

Having sorted that out, I spruced myself up and hit the town; actually I was just looking for somewhere to eat, I couldn't have 'hit' the town if I'd tried. My hunger sated, I hobbled back to the hotel via a small bar where I sampled a *grappa* or three.

In the hotel foyer, I caught a snippet of conversation between the receptionist and another guest; they were talking about *una isola,* an island, so I thought I'd check this out on my map. I also picked up a random selection of brochures that I hoped would soon send me to sleep if the *grappa* didn't kick in first.

In the Siracusa area my map was totally island-less, so I decided I'd misheard. On the other hand, many of the leaflets mentioned an island called Ortigia but it still took longer than it should have for me to have my 'Eureka' moment. A penny was ever so slowly dropping and as I cross-referenced this brochure with that brochure I gradually began to grasp the full picture. There were, in effect, two *Siracusa*s. There was, if you like, mainland Siracusa, the newer, boring bit and there was offshore Siracusa, Ortigia, the ancient island connected to the mainland by a short bridge. I had spent much of the afternoon wandering round the boring bit, not even realising that there was anything else to see. I did recall seeing signs to Ortigia but just thought it was another town up (or down) the coast.

The night was still young and I contemplated getting dressed and heading back out to explore but my feet needed a rest. Planning the next day's adventure, I fell asleep.

This was the day I fell in love with Siracusa, with all of it, even the aforementioned 'boring' bit. I followed the signs to Ortigia, no more than a fifteen-minute stroll away, and for the first time walked the fifty metres of the Ponte Umbertino, the bridge connecting the old with the new.

How do you describe somewhere that exudes so many wonderfully powerful sensations? For example, less than two hundred metres from the bridge, in the heart of the widest part of Ortigia, are the ruins of the Tempio di Apollo, dating from the 6th century BCE it's the oldest existing Doric temple in western Europe. This being Italy, it's at the junction of several roads, round the corner from a busy shopping street and across the way from one of the best produce markets I've ever seen. And that's only the beginning.

At every turn there's something to see but what is so special about Ortigia is not this or that building that has an entry in a guidebook (remember I didn't have a guide book), it's the compelling presence of everything, it's every building, every narrow street, every twist and turn ... the sense of the past is almost overwhelming as is the sense of decline and, in some parts, of decay. Arguably Ortigia is the one place where a guidebook is superfluous – off the beaten track was just as uplifting as many of the grander edifices. And although the spectre of derelict buildings and crumbling walls was all

Keeping the buildings of Ortigia apart

too often just around the corner, even these buildings, these *palazzi*, still exuded a curious elegance that I hoped one day might be restored.

Still buzzing from a day of sensory delights, I ate well and watched the sun set over the Mare Ionio, the Ionian Sea. On my way back to the hotel, along Ortigia's west-facing waterfront, I encountered an almost festive atmosphere with numerous stalls and hundreds of people enjoying a late evening walk. On reflection this was probably Ortigia's version of the *passeggiata* but at the time I didn't even know the word let alone recognise the signs. And if you don't know what I'm talking about ... then read on.

Back at Hotel Archimede I booked myself in for a third night and on the Sunday made a point of checking out some bed & breakfast accommodation in the heart of Ortigia for when (not if) I returned with Kay ('very soon ... very, very soon ... within the next fortnight or so').

And to think I had almost ended up in Catania which, I was later told, was a very narrow escape!

On the Monday, sad to have had to leave Siracusa so soon, I headed back to Messina. I parked the car in the queue for the ferry and made two calls: one to Paulo who said he and Jack would meet the ferry and the other to Capetti's to reserve a table for Kay and me the following evening ... to date the only booking they ever took from Sicily.

True to their word, Paulo and Jack were there when the ferry docked at Reggio and we drove up to Paulo's apartment for lunch. It was like the reunion of three old friends and, once again, Paulo conjured up a veritable feast before we drove a few kilometres north to the small coastal town of Scilla to join some of their friends for an afternoon *siesta* by the sea. In normal circumstances this would just not be my thing but I was both tired and excited about getting home and telling Kay about these few days so, on this occasion, I was happy to be the only pebble on the beach.

It was with gratitude and sadness that I said my goodbyes and headed further north to Lamezia Terme and the plane back to Stansted; I was not looking forward to the prospect of the two-hour drive to Bath.

Following in my own footsteps

Ten days later, on another Thursday afternoon, Kay and I fastened our seatbelts aboard the Ryanair flight to Lamezia Terme. I had been very persuasive and I think Kay went along with my plan just to keep me quiet. We were booked into a hotel by the airport for one night and the next day drove to Reggio and caught the ferry to Messina.

Within a couple of hours we were at the summit of Etna and this time I was wearing my socks. The guide looked at me and said something that I knew was a sign of recognition; I pointed to my socks and he smiled.

By late afternoon we were driving across the Ponte Umbertino and onto Ortigia where we stayed for three nights in the bed and breakfast on the Via Roma that I had checked out only a few days earlier.

We continued to retrace my steps and so it was compulsory for Kay to watch the sun set over the Mare Ionio as we ate and afterwards to wander around the stalls on the waterfront. She was very obliging and it was such a good feeling to share this place. We ended the evening doing something I hadn't done – we sat in the Piazza Archimede by the fountain, glass in hand, and watched the world go by.

Although I enjoyed showing Kay *my* Siracusa, we were now

equipped with a guidebook and a map and knew there was even more to this place than I had imagined. For example, up at the top of what I described earlier as the 'boring' end there was a Greek theatre and next to it a Roman amphitheatre. But this Teatro Greco was no ordinary tiered stone semicircle. Dating from the 5th century BCE, it is one of the oldest and most spectacular in the ancient Greek world.

But, this being Italy, the Teatro Greco is not just a thing of beauty to be revered and photographed; it is, above all else, a theatre and has been used as such every other year since 1914 to stage ancient Greek dramas first performed here over 2500 years previously. Once again it is difficult to imagine somewhere like Stonehenge or the Roman theatre at Verulamium (St Albans) being put to some practical use which actually *enhances* its status as an important part of the past.

Further up the coast nearer Etna, high up on a rocky plateau, is the town of Taormina where DH Lawrence once lived. Here too there is a younger Greek theatre (about the 2nd century BCE) where, yet again, plays continue to be staged ... though there are no plans to re-enact the gladiatorial combats that took place here when the Romans rebuilt it. Well, as far as we know, anyway.

We had a wonderful time in *our* Siracusa and never tired of wandering the streets and alleyways, some of which were so narrow that the local *carabinieri* had to use a Smart car. Two butch uniformed policemen sitting cheek-by-jowl in a Smart car is what cameras were made for ... sadly I couldn't focus fast enough as it shot round the corner in pursuit of nothing in particular!

We always had an eye open for future accommodation and stumbled upon a hotel undergoing renovation on the eastern side of Ortigia. Being nosey we went in to have a look and bumped into the Polish family who owned the building. They were very kind and showed us round the rooms that were already complete ... and instantly we knew this is where we'd stay next time. The Polish name of the hotel (Gutkowski) was a bit of a tongue-twister so, for us, it became, and remains, the Blue Hotel.

All too soon we were heading back towards Messina. As we passed Etna I tried to recall something I had read about likening Etna to a cat. I gave in and looked it up later. It was from the works of the Sicilian writer and politician Leonardo Sciascia who described the volcano as 'a huge house cat that purrs quietly and every so often awakens'. We didn't know it at the time but it wouldn't be long before it awoke with a vengeance.

Because the guidebook said we should, we stopped en route for a whistle-stop tour of Taormina; or rather we didn't stop because we couldn't find anywhere to park. So up the hill we went and nearly passed ourselves on the way back down again – next time it'll be less of a problem as I've now done the course on parking in Italy. Next time too, I'll buy a better guidebook, one that will be less coy about including a reference to two of the 20th century's most interesting (albeit controversial) writers, DH Lawrence and Truman Capote, both of whom used to live in Taormina *and* in the same villa, Fontana Vecchia*.

Before leaving Ortigia, I had called Paulo to ask him and Jack out to lunch, we were keen to repay their earlier kindnesses to me. He accepted and explained that Jack was now over in

---

* For the record I did buy another guide to Sicily but at the time forgot to check for references to Lawrence or Capote and then found out later that once again their time at Taormina had been airbrushed out ... what is it with these people?

Huffing and puffing atop Etna and at Villa del Casale

Sicily but that if I called him back when we got to Messina he'd meet the ferry.

True to his word, he was on the quayside waiting for us. I introduced him to Kay and he invited us up to his apartment to freshen up before we had lunch.

I suppose I should have smelt a rat ... but it never occurred to me that he had no intention of letting us take him out to lunch. Instead he was preparing another mega spread for us; yet again his hospitality knew no boundaries. The least we could do was give him a hand.

While I was in and out of the kitchen, Kay had cleared the table in the dining room looking out over the Straits of Messina. I had just started to bring in the food when Kay picked a piece of paper off the floor and put it on Paulo's desk but not before she noticed it was written in English.

Now, what would you have done? Of course she read it ... and she forced me to read it too. It was from Jack to Paulo. It was the story of broken trust and hurt, of a long friendship now ended; it was an angry and disappointed Jack saying his farewells to Paulo before leaving Reggio and heading for Sicily.

There you go ... I leave these two on their own for a couple of weeks and can they get on? No, they can not and now look what's happened!

We wondered whether or not we were meant to find Jack's note and, if we were, then how were we expected to react? It was all getting too complicated so we decided to return the note to the floor, ignore it and speak about Jack as if nothing had happened.

Another excellent lunch passed off with only the odd mention of Jack and all these were positive, whatever had happened here since my last visit was water under the bridge. Paulo, at least, had got over it.

By mid-afternoon we were heading for Scilla and another gathering on the beach though this time there was nowhere to park. So, double parked like a true Italian, we said our goodbyes to Paulo, thanked him for his presents (yes, lunch, sexual intrigue *and* presents) and headed for Lamezia.

We made one final call from the airport ... to Capetti's to reserve a table for the following evening ... to date the only booking they ever took from Calabria.

*

Later that year we kept our date with the people at the Blue Hotel and enjoyed another long weekend in Ortigia.

Although we revisited our favourite parts of the island, and always ended up in the Piazza Archimede in the late evening, this time we used it more as a base to explore other parts of the south and east of Sicily.

The highlight was a visit to the Villa del Casale which boasts what are judged to be among the most magnificent of all Roman mosaics ... and not only because it has what is believed to be the earliest record of a woman wearing a bikini! And, yet again, this breathtaking site was totally accessible even though excavations continue.

Thus far we had had no encounters with Sicily's dark side, the men in black. We didn't expect to. But two separate incidents fed our fertile imaginations and both happened on this visit, one in Siracusa close to the Teatro Greco and the other in a small village near the Villa del Casale.

On the first occasion what initially attracted our attention was the uniformity of the dress, the dark suits and the dark glasses, *Reservoir Dogs*-style. Then it was where they sat. It was a hot day, everyone was feeling it and yet this group chose to be tucked away in an airless corner with walls on three sides. They were not being loud – normally men together argue politics or *calcio* (football) and it's not normally the Italian way to talk quietly. They were of a certain age, nobody young, nobody old. There was a 'leader' to whom they all paid respect, particularly one nervous late-comer.

We watched subtly but intently looking for clues, trying to pick up a word or two ... like *vendetta* or *testa di cavallo* (horse's head). Perhaps we were falling for the stereotype, perhaps, after all, this was the impromtu AGM of the local disposable nappy salesmen and they were so embarrassed that they spoke quietly and wore dark glasses to remain incognito. Whatever, whoever, it didn't matter – we enjoyed the speculation.

Our second 'encounter' with our imaginations was when we stopped off for a drink en route to Messina from Villa del Casale. Most places were closed (yet again we'd hit the *siesta*) but there was one bar open. Four men sat round a table talking and gesturing loudly. They nodded to us as we made for the counter where I ordered an *espresso* and Kay a hot chocolate. The man of the house appeared to be all fingers and thumbs when he came to make the chocolate and his wife had to take over and sort it out.

We sat down and, as is our wont, tried to tap in to the men's conversation – not to deliberately eavesdrop but as a way of gauging whether or not our grasp of the language had improved or not. When Italian men talk their hands inevitably become an integral part of the conversation; but these hands were different – at least three of them had a finger missing. We couldn't quite make out whether it was the same finger or whether or not the fourth member of the group was all in one piece ... but it didn't matter, it set us wondering.

The obvious answer was that there was some occupation hereabouts that could result in the loss of a finger or two; but how could so many men be so careless? A more intriguing, but less likely, solution to such carelessness was that it was something to do with you-know-who. The index finger has an important status in mafia lore and figures in the initiation ceremony when it is pricked or cut and the blood smeared on the image of a saint. Or, of course, it could have been genetic and they were all brothers or cousins.

This was Sicily and, given the history, you're entitled to indulge in the odd bit of speculation. But if our enquiring minds could only come up with a few men in a bar, a few whispered words and a few missing fingers, then I think it's safe to say that, relatively speaking, *La Cosa Nostra* is keeping more of a low profile these days.

Fingers crossed.

As we returned once again to Calabria and said our farewells to Sicily, we knew we had one piece of unfinished business in Siracusa – one day we were going to sit in the Teatro Greco, in the early evening sun, and watch a Greek play.

And eventually we did ... and even now the memory of it leaves me breathless.

Sardinia – an optical illusion

Every year in late March and late September, Kay and I go away for anything up to a week or ten days. It's our respective birthdays and if we're away it stops people feeling duty-bound to shower us with gifts.

It was late summer and I was trawling the internet trying to find somewhere to stay in the Italian island of Sardinia in September, preferably somewhere off the beaten track. I had already booked the Ryanair flights from London Stansted to Alghero in the north-west and acquired a couple of guide books. I was looking for somewhere central from where we could explore the whole island but drew a blank. So I edged my mouse towards the west coast and eventually came up with a bed & breakfast, La Meridiana del Sole, in a small inland town called Scano di Montiferro.

The day before we left I had expected to pick up a new pair of glasses, the ones I was wearing were held together with fuse wire and were unlikely to last much longer. My optician got it wrong and my new ones failed to arrive and so I stepped off the plane in Alghero wearing my attractive fuse-wire designer specs, now miraculously turning themselves into sunglasses. I had an emergency roll of fuse-wire in my pocket.

Isola Maddalena

Témpio
Pausánia

OLBIA

Tavolara

Sássari

Alghero

Siniscola

Orosei

Bosa

Macomér

●Nuoro

○**SCANO DI MONTIFERRO**

Grotta di
Ispinigoli

Cuglieri

SARDINIA

Oristano

Cagliari

Tyrrhenian
Sea

Cagliari to Oristano · 95km

It was an early flight so we decided to spend what was left of the morning exploring Alghero before having lunch and heading down the coast towards Scano. We found a tourist-less café and tucked into a couple of slices of pizza and a cold drink when, innocently, I took off my glasses, wiped my eyes and then tried to clean the lenses on the bottom of my T-shirt … need I go on?

I'd broken them again and wasn't sure if fuse wire was going to work this time but somehow I managed to cobble things together even though I knew the only thing in sight was the end. The problem was that these were varifocals, each lens being three lenses – driving/computer/reading – and, of course, they were my sunglasses.

The winding coast road south, perched precariously between mountain and sea, was glorious and surprisingly free of traffic for such a magnificent setting. We wound down to Bosa before cutting inland and south east towards Tresnurághes, Sennariolo and finally Scano where we arrived, as arranged, about four in the afternoon; we parked up and started to look for La Meridiana del Sole. After about ten fruitless minutes we found ourselves in a small *piazza*, we stopped a local lad and, summoning up our best Italian, asked, '*Dov'è* La Meridiana del Sole?' He turned round and pointed, we were standing about five metres from the door.

In vain, we knocked the door with varying degrees of brutality; an elderly woman, dressed in black from head to toe, emerged from the house opposite and shuffled over to speak to us, making no allowances for the fact that we might not speak any Italian. But we got the gist of it … he (Angelo) had left and was in Cagliari working. Having delivered the good news she shrugged her shoulders and slowly retraced her steps and closed the door on what happened next.

As one door shut, another opened … it was the door to

the right of 'our' door, it was the door of the Pro Loco, a sort of tourist information centre, opening (a little late) for the post-siesta session. The Pro Loco was manned by two women (if that's possible), one of whom said "*Meridiana*?" with a definite question mark at the end. We nodded in broken Italian and she raised a restraining finger, said "*Un attimo*", stuck her *cellulare* to her ear, made a call then looked at us and said "*Cinque minuti*".

Five minutes later there was a screeching of rubber as a battered Fiat Uno shot round the corner, came to a halt and deposited a nervous young woman at our feet. Trying to regain her composure while adjusting her glasses and re-arranging her dark curly hair, she introduced herself as Rina and in passable English explained the problem. Well, actually, she explained, now that she was here, there wasn't a problem.

Angelo, a painter of stage scenery (we think that's what she said), had indeed taken up some last-minute work in Cagliari and, as we were booked in for bed and breakfast while he was away, he had found a much more attractive substitute in the only available out-of-work English speaker in Scano.

Rina took us into the house and showed us round. There were three bedrooms upstairs so we had a choice; there was a living room, a dining room and a kitchen though the latter was Rina's territory as she would be coming in each morning to make and serve us breakfast, *la prima colazione*.

She was very eager to please and kept apologising for her poor English – if we spoke Italian as well as she spoke English we'd have considered ourselves fluent! While she was explaining something or other to Kay, I noticed something about Rina and got very excited. I reached for the phrasebook and the dictionary ... I had to get this right. I practised it in my head. I waited for a break in the conversation ...

"*C'è un ottico a Scano?*" I said, pointing first to Rina's glasses and then to my botched repair job.

"*A Scano, no. A Cuglieri però … ottica Dory Perria a Cuglieri*", she replied, clearly astounded at my Italian.

"*È lontano?*" I was on a roll.

"*No, non è lontano, sei kilometri.*" I wondered whether these were six Italian kilometres which always seemed much longer.

"*Aperto domani?*" I had nearly used up all my Italian words.

"*Si, alle nove e mezzo.*"

Rina went on to sing the praises of the local optician, Dory Perria, and assured me that she could sort me out. So, problem solved, all I had to do was turn up at Dory Perria's place in Cuglieri at half nine the following morning and, hey presto, I'd leave with a new pair of specs. I don't think so.

In the meantime we had to find somewhere to eat. Rina told us that there were six bars in Scano but that none of them really offered food; I think she was seeing the tourist in us, she didn't realise we were now locals and didn't need or want a tourist menu. So she directed us to a new cliff-top restaurant, so new in fact that it was accessible only by a road that hadn't been built yet. She was right, the food was good and I can safely say that the road, such as it was, was a total nightmare … it was the same on the way back except that it was in the dark and we met another vehicle coming in the opposite direction. We decided that next time we'd find somewhere a little closer, a little more accessible, a little kinder to the car.

Next morning I woke and switched on the bedside lamp I'd 'borrowed' from one of the other rooms. Nothing, the bulb had gone. I got out of bed and switched on the main light. Nothing. Kay tried her lamp. Again nothing. Clearly there was no electricity.

Still, no problem, we could hear Rina downstairs preparing breakfast. Might not be any coffee, but we could cope. We took our time washing and dressing, giving Rina as much time as possible to solve the problem. We went down to the kitchen and got the feeling that, yes, now there was light. And there was.

I think Rina had acquired every candle in Scano and covered almost every available surface with them; there were thin ones, fat ones, coloured ones and scented ones and they were all lit. As the dining room was downstairs in a window-less basement there was little natural light except from the kitchen which did have an outside door and a window.

Rina explained how she'd arrived earlier and discovered the lack of electricity and that she didn't want to spoil our first morning in Sardinia ... so she panicked and called Angelo in Cagliari who suggested a breakfast that didn't require electricity. Still in panic mode, the candlelit bit was Rina's idea ... nevertheless it was much appreciated and we'll never forget our first breakfast in Sardinia.

Sardinia does not get the same press as Sicily. There are obvious reasons for this – no mafia, no Etna and no Greek theatres or temples. DH Lawrence described the island as being 'lost between Europe and Africa and belonging to nowhere'.

So we were hoping and expecting to find something different here. We loved the energy of Sicily but guessed that the quieter pace here might suit us too. In 1960, in his book *South to Sardinia*, Alan Ross predicted that visitors would 'go on increasing ... for this is an island, under-sold for so long, that amply repays the extra effort of getting there'.

Well, we had made that extra effort and as we set off for Cuglieri that first morning, my glasses still flaunting their delicate fuse-wire bandage and perched precariously between nose and ear, I was fervently hoping that the legendary Dory Perria was going to come up with some sort of miracle. I had a plan and I knew that what I was going to ask of her was something that no optician in Bath would do.

Of course, not wishing to make a spectacle of myself, I swotted up and rehearsed all the words relating to being 'At the Opticians' and, the moment we stopped outside the premises of Ottica Dory Perria, I forgot the lot. It was just as well her shop was *chiuso* (closed).

We had met an American in Umbria who claimed, after years of dedicated research, that *chiuso* was the most common Italian word. He had probably suffered the scourge of the *siesta* but it is true that even outside the *siesta* shutdown, there are still many *chiuso* signs around, particularly when you're about to run out of petrol.

I digress ... back to Cuglieri.

It was time to regroup, find a bar, have a *caffè* and consult the phrasebook. Twenty minutes later we returned to the shop ... it was open, but packed. We sat down and awaited our turn.

At last we had Dory Perria's undivided attention and I asked her if she spoke English. As she shook her head I took off my glasses and handed them to her. She guessed the fuse wire was an added extra and removed it, trying to hide a giggle as she did so. She told me they were beyond repair, *non si può ripararli.* That bit I think I already knew.

Deep breath ... now for the rehearsed bit. I was trying to say that my glasses had three lenses when she looked at me, held the glasses up to the light, and summed it all up in a single word, *varifocali.* We were talking the same language after all, but not for long.

Between us Kay and I managed to get across the next bit. We wanted Dory Perria to find a pair of frames into which she could put my lenses. Now this was more complicated than it sounds: I knew she would never find an exact match so she'd have to come up with something slightly smaller and regrind the lenses to fit while making sure the centre point remained more or less in the centre.

She agreed and so together we started the search for suitable frames. We found some that would have worked but for the bridge being too wide or too narrow, but eventually we came up with the answer.

She took the frames and indicated that she'd have to go to her workshop at the back of the shop and suggested we return in an hour.

An hour or so later we emerged from a small shop in a small town, on the top of a hill, in the middle of nowhere, on an 'undersold' island. Dory Perria had done the business. I was sporting my new designer specs and carrying my free gift, a lens cleaner that resembled a pen. It had cost me €60 (about £40 at the time). I couldn't wait to get back to Bath and wave them at the optician who hadn't managed to deliver my new pair before I went on holiday.

I always take my special Dory Perria glasses with me on holiday … they are my emergency pair.

Making friends with families

It was our second night in Scano and we had no intention of reprising the late-night, off-road adventure of the night before; we wanted to eat locally, preferably adjacent to a tarmacked thoroughfare. So we began to work our way round the town's six bars. We found four, none of which served food.

Approaching the fifth, on a road heading out of town, we could just make out a sign hanging over a footpath. As we got closer we read the word 'pizzeria' and began to get excited but when we actually got there we could see it was an old sign and that this was probably just another food-less bar. By this time we were thirsty so we decided to have a drink and, if all else failed, we could drive the six kilometres back to Cuglieri where we'd spotted a small restaurant earlier in the day.

The bar counter was to the left of the door but there was another room to the right with tables and chairs but no people and no indication that anyone was expected. We ordered two glasses of red wine and sat by the bar to await developments. Nothing happened so we asked if it was possible to eat. The barman said, "*Un attimo*", and disappeared only to reappear a few moments later to continue serving other customers at the bar.

Then she appeared. She stood, arms folded, framed in the entrance to the table-and-chairs room ... I half expected that she would be enveloped in smoke rising from the floor. She was tall, elegant and slender for her age, mid-50s I would have guessed, but she had that old-fashioned headmistress demeanour. She seemed capable of putting you across her knee at the drop of a hat. And yet ... perhaps we just caught sight of a twinkle in her eye.

She focused on us (perhaps she's admiring my new glasses, I thought) and waited for us to make the first move. Kay broke the silence and asked if we could eat, "*Possiamo mangiare?*". The woman continued to scrutinise us, looking us up and down and eventually said, "*Sì*". She directed us to a table in the corner.

As ever we chose to drink red wine but we had no choice about what we ate, pork was all she had. She disappeared into the kitchen to prepare our meal from scratch, without a microwave or a packet; every vegetable we ate came from her garden, as did the fruit. We ate like royalty.

This woman was a great cook and we booked ourselves in, same time, same place the following night ... and every night thereafter though we knew we'd have to find an alternative on the Wednesday when, according to the notice on the door, they were closed all day.

Between the four of us, Kay and me, Nuncia, the cook, and her husband Pietro, the barman, we had bits and pieces of five languages: not surprisingly Nuncia and Pietro spoke Italian, Nuncia also spoke some French and German, Pietro spoke some Portuguese; As well as English, Kay and I spoke some French, some Portuguese and some Italian; but I was best with German. Somehow we got by.

Now that Nuncia was expecting us she would check with us the night before that we were happy with what she was going to prepare for the following night. She was on a roll and the meals increased in quality, quantity and variety as the days went by. Once again we had hit the jackpot but the best was still to come.

When we weren't eating and drinking with Nuncia and Pietro we were breakfasting with Rina. The electrical problem had been solved and never happened again, so no more candlelit breakfasts for us. Angelo remained in Cagliari.

Rina was warming to her role and revelling in the kudos of looking after the only English people in Scano (in fact the only foreigners in Scano) and her English improved day by day while our Italian, being on a lower trajectory, was only improving year by year.

Scano was a small, tidy, non-pretentious town, haphazardly scattered on the side of a low hill and home to just under a thousand people. Unlike Monterchi with its Madonna del Parto it had no real claim to fame, this was not a place that in itself was likely to sweep passing tourists off their feet. In making his home available as a bed & breakfast and putting up engaging signs on every approach road, Angelo had shown a modicum of enterprise and optimism. For most people this would have been, at best, a passing-through place but for us it was somewhere we could call 'home' while we explored other parts of Sardinia. We just didn't 'do' travelling round to a different bed every night, unpacking and repacking. And I'm pretty sure Angelo never anticipated that anyone would ever stay at La Meridiana del Sole for as long as we did.

Being the only foreigners in Scano and being around for ten days or so, meant that most people in the town were aware of us. We always said *buon giorno* or *buonasera* when we passed people in the street or saw them in cafés or shops. Shortly before we left Scano we were talking to Rina about her mother and mentioned that we were sorry we hadn't met

Yours truly propping up a favourite mural in Scano

her. Rina explained that we had met her – apparently on the previous day at the local market we had said good morning to her. She knew who we were but, of course, at the time we didn't know her.

So Rina was a happy bunny and asked us out for a late-night drink at one of the bars so that we could meet her special friend Stellina. We arranged to meet at the bed & breakfast as Rina said that this particular bar was not easy to find. We guessed it was the sixth, the one that still eluded us.

It was. We would never have found it. It was just after half ten at night and the three of us were walking down a narrow street that Kay and I had been up and down many times. Rina stopped at a house, opened the door and we entered a cross between a front room and a bar, peopled mainly by the young. It was quite different from all the other bars in Scano, not just because it didn't have a name over the door and didn't look remotely like a bar from the outside, but because, like Nuncia's, it was less plastic, more of a real place. Stellina and her friends were here and there were introductions all round which gave us the opportunity to try out our two new words.

Hitherto both Kay and I had owned up to being 'English' but that wasn't quite right. So, in the nameless bar, we confessed: I said "*Sono irlandese*" and Kay said "*Sono gallese*". Everyone now knew the awful truth, I was Irish and Kay was Welsh and it has to be said everyone seemed very pleased for us.

The beer and wine flowed and it was well after midnight when we put our new nationalities to bed.

Next morning we decided to repay Rina for our late night detour into Scano sub-culture and asked her if she'd like to eat with us at Nuncia's that evening. She said she couldn't so we asked what evening would suit. Again she said she couldn't by which she did not mean that it was inconvenient, she meant that Nuncia's was somewhere she could not, would not, go.

What we didn't realise until then was that Nuncia and Rina were related. Nuncia was Rina's *zia*, her aunt. Pietro and Rina's father were *fratelli*, brothers. And there was a family feud, *una vendetta*.

Typical ... the two people we know best in Scano are at loggerheads over some family dispute though, that said, the 'problem' did appear to be one-way. Nuncia would have been happy to cook for and eat with Rina, but Rina wouldn't eat with Nuncia.

We never did get to the bottom of it – although that, as you'll see, didn't stop us speculating – other than knowing it had its roots in some sort of falling out between the two brothers; Rina clearly felt that Pietro was in the wrong and that she needed to support her father. It must be said that Rina felt no animosity towards Nuncia.

From our point of view it never affected our relationship with either. In a sense Nuncia had no part in it and I suspect if we had ever brought the subject up she would have just shrugged her shoulders and said something like, 'Well that's Sardinians for you' ... Nuncia hailed from Ischia, an island off the mainland coast near Naples not far from Capri (see map on page 174).

Reconnoitring and revelling in Scano

In between breakfasting with Rina and eating with *la zia e lo zio*, we were exploring Sardinia.

We drove north east to Sassari, Sardinia's second city and returned via the coast and Alghero where we again wandered round the alleyways and shops in the Old Town. We liked it here in and around the battlements and towers with the sea on three sides and the picturesque harbour to the north. Alghero has a strong Spanish tradition and apparently some of the older locals are bilingual, their second language being Italian and their first a version of Catalan. But things change and traditions die out as new generations, influenced increasingly by the sights and sounds of a tele-visual world, embrace their present. Although we returned several times to Alghero we never did hear anyone speak anything but Italian.

We went south towards Oristano and stopped off at a couple of deserted beaches and then headed for Oristano itself, the capital of the province of the same name. As capitals go it was a big disappointment but that was really our fault for, yet again, we had arrived in the middle of the *siesta*.

On another day we went even further south to Sardinia's capital, Cagliari, where we soon found ourselves in the ideal spot to watch the world go by, in among the porticos of *Via*

Roma, overlooking the harbour and the huge ships that link the island with mainland Italy, Sicily and Africa. As the *siesta* crept across the city we headed in from the seafront to the Bastione San Remy and climbed the magnificent staircase to take in the breathtaking views of the city and its waterfront from the top of the ramparts. We continued our climb along the narrow empty streets toward the Castello Quarter and on to the Cittadella dei Musei, the city's museum district. We were hungry and in this land of simple, nourishing fare ended up at the only place in Italy that goes in for pre-packed microwaved Italian food. What a disappointment, the food that is, not Cagliari, definitely not Cagliari.

We also traversed the island to Nuoro which we expected to be *chiuso* as it was a Sunday but the bars and cafés were open and we spent a delightful hour or so sitting in the sun with the locals, mostly men, in the Piazza San Giovanni before we headed further east towards the coast and the Grotta di Ispinigoli.

The Grotta di Ispinigoli is a network of underground caves at the heart of which is a thirty-eight metre stalagmite, the tallest in Europe. Definitely worth seeing ... guided parties left to descend every half hour ... except for about two hours around the *siesta* ... and we arrived one minute too late! The last pre-*siesta* party was descending into the depths, the ticket office was closing its shutters, no exceptions were being made. And we had a couple of hours to kill.

So we headed for the coast, past the dramatic marble quarries on the slopes of Monte Tuttavista near Orosei – raw scars on the landscape that somehow were beautiful and ugly at the same time. We had lunch on the never-ending beach at Marina di Orosei and lay in the sun, the beach to ourselves ... until, that is, a family with about eight children and a *füssball* decided that the best place to sit on this empty beach was right next to us ... luckily we had an appointment elsewhere.

Back at the Grotta we were first in the queue, though sometimes it's difficult to tell in Italy as queues often go sideways instead of in a line, and soon we were heading underground. We followed our guide down narrow, steep steps and across well-lit galleries and around cascades of stalagmites and stalactites showing off their almost translucent colours and hues. I tried to imagine what it would have been like for the people who first saw these shapes and colours by flickering torchlight. Every formation was spectacular but the one we were here to see was stunning; it wasn't just the size, it was the setting at the centre of a huge echoing cavern and it was the way it was lit. Jaws dropped as our guide went into overdrive with all the relevant statistics. Shutterbugs twisted and turned, crouched and stretched, desperate to get a better shot than the postcard. I often find photographing the postcard itself on the rack outside the shop gives you the best shot.

Had our Italian been better, we would probably have heard our guide explain about the deep chasm below the stalagmite and a natural altar ... And what did people do with natural altars and deep chasms in days of yore to make sure they got a mention on some future guided tour? Why, they sacrificed virgins, of course! The guide directed our gaze down into the so-called Pozzo delle Vergine – literally the well of the virgins but sometimes referred to more dramatically as the virgin's abyss. And, you know, it could have been true ... the well and the altar overseen by a thirty-eight metre phallic God dancing to a flickering light.

We were tired after our day out east and so were glad to get back to Scano and freshen up before heading for Nuncia's.

It was Sunday evening, the bar was busier than usual and in the dining room nearly every table, including 'ours', was occupied. But Nuncia was ahead of the game and had kept us another table in the corner by the entrance to and from the bar.

It turned out to be one of those memorable evenings where there is a lot of loudness and laughing and everyone in the room seems to be involved in everyone else's conversations. Apart from us, most seemed to know each other but we were soon part of the group even if our Italian was not always up to the job. Nuncia's sons, Ricardo and Salvatore were both there too lending a hand.

We had finished our meal and I was trying to explain to someone at the next table that he looked like Elton John, as you do, when a head shot round the door, an Italian head that I'd never seen before, and said in English 'Hello Niall?'. Yes, there was definitely a question mark at the end.

I have to admit that this threw me for a few seconds. My mind did that thing that you sometimes see at railway stations or on Wall Street when the information flips over and over as it re-programmes. I took a stab in the dark and said, 'Ciao, Angelo?'

It was the only rational solution. Somebody who knew we'd be eating at Nuncia's (a call to Rina). Somebody we'd never seen before but knew us and knew my name. Somebody who spoke some English. And someone (Pietro) to point out where we were sitting. It could only be Angelo.

And it was. He'd travelled up from Cagliari to say hello and to see that we were happy with everything at his house but would be returning the next day. Can you think of any other excuse for an impromptu party?

Angelo sat down and was joined by his friend the local hairdresser, a Freddie Mercury look-a-like – I joke you not – and, well, I don't think either of us recall much after that, except that Angelo invited us to have *il pranzo*, lunch, with him the next day at the house. It was all a blur, memorable but not much remembered, though I think we were pretty convinced that both Elton John and Freddie Mercury were there.

On Tuesday evening we ate as usual at Nuncia's and afterwards she joined us for a *liquore*, *grappa* for me and *limoncello* for Kay. We said we'd see her on Thursday (the bar being shut on Wednesday) when Nuncia said, "*No, domani voi mangiate a casa nostra*". By saying we'd eat with them, we assumed they weren't closing after all but, no, the bar would close as usual and we were invited to eat with them as guests of the family. We would eat at eight.

We weren't sure of the etiquette for such occasions but decided to take chocolates and a bottle of Irish whisky that I'd already bought to take home for myself. Of course, we now know that a gift that goes down well in such circumstances is a large *torta*, a cake preferably with lots and lots of cream.

We were slightly nervous when we arrived at the bar which was closed to locals but open to us; it didn't seem quite right. We knocked the door and an altogether different Nuncia ushered us in; this was the Nuncia at home, not the Nuncia at work.

She had to get back to the kitchen so Pietro was delegated to became our temporary host; he grabbed a torch and we followed him outside and down some steps and into his own personal hide-away, a *cantina*, a place to make, and taste, wine.

We realised then that Pietro must have made the wine we had been drinking with our meals but he wanted to share some others with us, an *aperitivo*, a couple of whites, a red or three and naturally we took the tasting very seriously – first of all we had a whiff of the bouquet, then made reassuring sounds of approval before swirling it round a little and then

The ruin of a typical Sardinian *nuraghe*

down it went ... we decided not to do that spitting out bit as it might seem impolite. He also told us he made *grappa* and *limoncello* and showed us the still that he said was his brother's. Kay and I gave each other a knowing look, we had both gone down the same track and wondered whether the still was the cause of the brothers' feud?

Nuncia summoned us back to the bar where the *antipasto* was already on the table and we were joined by one of her sons, Ricardo (Salvatore worked away during the week). Nuncia had gone for the full monty: *antipasto*, *primo piatto*, *secundo piatto*, *dolce* and *liquore*, a real Italian feast.

Apart from the meat and fish, everything that Nuncia cooked for her extended family that evening was from her own garden: courgettes, broad beans, aubergines, tomatoes, onions, peppers, garlic, asparagus, herbs and olives and those in season and not from the freezer would have been gathered in fresh that day. And none of this was for our benefit, this was how the family ate day in and day out but, as ever with eating in Italy, they took their time, so it was well past ten before the last plates were cleared away.

But the alcohol continued to flow and, as it did, everyone's command of their various second and third languages (Italian, German, French, Portuguese and English) got better. I recall putting together one sentence that contained four different languages and then made matters worse by trying to explain what I'd just done. A few moments later I turned to Kay and said something in French ... she looked bemused and reminded me that I could actually speak to her in English.

With tongues loosening I couldn't resist taking this opportunity to remind Nuncia about our first evening here and asked her what she was thinking when we first asked to eat. She laughed and admitted that she was indeed eyeing us up, deciding whether or not she liked us enough to cook for us. She decided she did and the rest, as they say, is gastronomic history.

A memorable evening was coming to an end but before we staggered back to base Nuncia took us through to the back of the bar and opened the door into a bedroom, "*La prossima volta dovete stare qui*" she said proudly. This was a little more than a mere invitation: the next time we came to Scano, then this is where we *would* stay.

For obvious reasons we wanted a quiet Thursday so we retreated to our own, almost private, *nuraghe* to sit in the sun.

The *nuraghi* are a Sardinian phenomenon; these squat circular towers are everywhere on the Sardinian landscape, over 7000 of them, more than double the estimated number in 1960! They represent a civilisation dating from around 1800BCE to 500BCE and didn't seem peculiar to any particular area or terrain. Because of its position, you could assume 'ours' was some sort of look-out tower (and maybe it was) but that didn't explain all the ones in low-lying areas, in fields, on hillsides, in clusters, with or without fortifications. It almost seems that there is a different explanation for each *nuraghe* ... perhaps there is no explanation that covers them all other than their basic structure.

On the seaward side of Tresnurághes we had discovered a track that seemed interesting and just followed it on and on and on until it ended by a *nuraghe* on a headland at the top of a cliff, There was always one other car there belonging to the two men who were slowly restoring it (the tower, not the car) and they didn't seem to mind us being about ... a nod and a *buon giorno* seemed to be enough to establish diplomatic relations.

So this became 'our' *nuraghe*, a clandestine retreat in an isolated ancient landscape overlooking the sea. Nobody else ever came here. Other than the restorers and whoever employed them, I doubt many knew it was there.

Our time was nearly up and we did the round of goodbyes. Nuncia and Rina made sure that we left Scano with reminders of our time there and one of these, a coffee and orange *liquore* from Rina's mother, was simply exquisite, *squisito*, and since then we've never been without a bottle or two at home.

We told Nuncia and Rina that we would return though we had no idea when; at the back of our minds we still had other parts of Sardinia to visit, especially the north-east around Olbia.

Two things focused our attention on keeping our promise: one was that we were fast running out of that golden elixir that Rina's mother had given us and the second was a run-in with an unexpected bit of culture courtesy of David Herbert Lawrence.

SEA AND SARDINIA

By D. H. LAWRENCE

Jan Juta

Illustrated
with 8 pictures in full color
by JAN JUTA
and with a map of Sardinia by the author.

The front cover of the first edition of *Sea and Sardinia*, published in 1921

Let it be Sardinia ... again

Richard Aldington, a biographer of DH Lawrence, said the two books that bring the reader to Lawrence at his most accessible are *Sons and Lovers* and *Sea and Sardinia*.

Lawrence wrote *Sea and Sardinia* following a nine-day excursion that he and his wife Frieda, whom he called the queen bee, made to the island from their Taormina home in Sicily in January 1921 ... and I trawled through the local second-hand bookstores until I found a copy.

A restless Lawrence felt the need to get away from Sicily, possibly even to move permanently, and mulled over several possible destinations for his trip before narrowing it down to Spain or Sardinia. He then makes his choice, 'Sardinia, which has no history, no date, no race, no offering. Let it be Sardinia.' On his return to Sicily he wrote *Sea and Sardinia* entirely from memory in six weeks.

The book is written in the present tense, a breathless running commentary on the six days he took to travel between Cagliari and Nuoro and on to Terranova Pausanias (he normally drops the 'Pausanias') mainly by train and bus; almost half the book deals with getting to Cagliari from Taormina and from Terranova back to Sicily.

As ever, I read the book with a map to hand – something

which the perceptive Lawrence supplied free of charge for readers of the first edition – and tried in vain to locate this place called Terranova. I couldn't find it because it didn't exist as such; it was Olbia, the name Terranova having been ditched in the 1940s at the end of the Mussolini era.

It was a fascinating read and, assuming the narrow-guage railway he took continued to operate, I hoped one day that I might be able to retrace his steps. In the meantime I was keen to get back and explore that north-east corner around Olbia, the region known as Gallura.

Six months on and another Ryanair flight later we were back in the sun at Alghero, back in the Old Town. We had time to kill before we set off to meet our new hostess, Monica, on the outskirts of Olbia.

On the face of it the arrangement appeared uncomplicated. There was, Monica explained in her email, a BP petrol station on the left hand side of the main road from Sassari to Olbia, just on the outskirts of the town. We would meet there at five, she'd be in a grey Fiat Panda. Simple enough … but then this was to be an Italian rendezvous and, as we were to discover on other occasions, there can sometimes be an unforseen element thrown into the mix.

We arrived at the outskirts of Olbia ten minutes early and passed an Agip station but no BP and soon found ourselves in the town itself. So we drove back out and tried again; we thought we must have missed it or perhaps it was down a side road on the left. But no BP station. We wondered if there was another road from Sassari and stopped to consult the map; another route was possible but unlikely. We went back into Olbia, and into the jaws of the early evening rush hour, but still no BP station. It had gone a quarter past five.

We drove out again and decided to go back ten kilometres

in case Monica's 'outskirts' began further out of town than we had thought. As we were passing the Agip station, I caught a glimpse of a woman getting into a grey car and did a dodgy, Italian-style, u-turn and crossed into the station forecourt. The woman was about to drive off until I blocked her exit.

'Monica?' I enquired hopefully as she got out of her car. She nodded.

I asked what had happened to the BP station; she looked up at the Agip sign and with a shrug of the shoulders said, 'Must have changed. I haven't been here for a while.'

We marvelled at her coolness faced with the fact that she almost literally lost two clients. Still, all was well, we had found each other and that was the main thing.

The plan for these few days in Sardinia was simple: fly to Alghero, stay four nights in Olbia at Monica's, drive to Scano and stay with Nuncia for four nights and then back to Alghero for a night. Our first day back in Scano would also be Kay's birthday.

So far, so good. We followed Monica to her house, an attractive low, modern building set in a well-kept, private garden just out of town. It was spring, everything back home was about to burst forth but here we had a garden full of flowers already strutting their stuff. We were welcomed by five or six *gatti*, cats of various ages and doubtful parentage; no problem, we had two cats of our own. Monica showed us to our room and invited us to join her for a cup of tea after we'd settled in.

We sat with Monica as she took us through everything ... keys, where we could sit in the garden, the best places to eat, where to go, what to do, her library of books, brochures and maps ... and breakfast.

Monica, it seemed, was not a morning person; she was a

late riser, a bed & breakfast hostess who didn't do breakfasts in the conventional sense. So, she explained, she would prepare breakfast the night before and leave it out for us, and this included coffee in a vacuum flask and everything else we would need. We could live with that.

She also mentioned that the cats were not normally allowed in the house and that a couple of the younger ones were not fully potty-trained, so we might stumble upon the odd 'offering' in the garden. So we'd watch our step.

Monica told us about *un ristorante particolare* and phoned them for us but it was fully booked so, instead, she reserved a table for us there the following night. She then called her second favourite and booked us in for dinner that evening and gave us directions to both. We returned to our room to get ready for the evening. We felt worn out; Monica's induction had lasted over an hour and a half.

The next morning we awoke to an eerie silence from within the house and the protestations of cats on the outside.

As instructed, we made for the dining area and helped ourselves to an unsupervised breakfast. Suffice to say it was different. Unusually for Italy everything was pre-packed; pre-packed bread roll, pre-packed croissant, pre-packed *biscotti*, pre-packed jam and pre-packed butter. And, of course, pre-prepared coffee. Not the best breakfast in the world but nor was it the worst coffee.

All this was accompanied by the morning chorus of cats' claws scraping down glass in a vain attempt to enter the forbidden zone. There was also a whiff in the air, a whiff of something different ... familiar but from a distant past. Maybe when we went outside, we'd remember. And we did.

It was cat shit.

Now, as even cat-haters know, cats are normally fastidiously clean. When all that lovely cat food emerges from the other end, they have the decency to find somewhere to dig a hole, drop it in and cover it; usually next door. They can even be trained to use a household toilet though, as far as I am aware, they haven't mastered the flushing bit. They certainly don't head for the nearest bit of concrete or the nearest wall and deposit it all in a pile for the world to see.

But they did here.

And it wasn't just one or two of the younger ones. It seemed as if they all did it. And there weren't five or six, there were at least eight, maybe more, it was difficult to tell. It was cat-shit anarchy!

But we were off for the day, so we assumed it would be cleared up by the time we got back – as it clearly had been the evening before. And anyway we hadn't planned being around the house other than first thing in the morning and early evening, so it wasn't *cat*astrophic.

Over the next few days we explored Gallura, from the aquamarine waters of the Costa Smeralda, to the rugged northern coastline with views across to French Corsica, from the Isola Maddalena to the winding mountainous roads around Tempio Pausania. We never ventured south of Olbia as we would be travelling that way on our way down to Scano.

Each of these was memorable in its own way: the colour of the sea along the Costa Smeralda that no photograph could recreate; Kay's exploding smoothie bottle as we sat on a rocky cliff-top eyeing up Corsica; taking the ferry to Isola Maddalena and sitting overlooking the sea listening to a surreal American briefing on the war in Afghanistan – we were right below the US/NATO base here and the car radio picked up a rogue signal; and the UN World Water Day march through Tempio Pausania, not because there was even such an event here but because of the huge numbers of people, mainly families, that participated.

And, of course, despite our unexpected rush-hour brush with Olbia that first evening, we returned to explore Gallura's largest town one of the area's two administrative centres, Tempio Pausania being the other. This was my first opportunity to compare and contrast with the Lawrence experience of 1921 but then I remembered that he shot through Terranova (as it then was) like a dose of salts – he wanted to be out of this place, he wanted to catch the steamer to Civitavecchia on the Italian mainland north of Rome. In his rush down to the harbour and after 'bumping and rattling down a sombre, uncouth, barren-seeming street', he observed that Terranova '... felt more like a settlement than a town'.

Well, you'll be pleased to know that, eighty years on and with a new name (Olbia is, in fact, its original Greek name meaning 'happy', Terranova was the usurper), the town has come of age. The 'barren-seeming' streets are long gone and in their place is the normal hustle and bustle of Italian café-culture and modern *negozi* (shops); the telegraph office that Lawrence visited is probably an internet café now.

True, most roads still seem to head down to the harbour but, instead of the 'bunch of dark masts' that Lawrence espied, there are the huge, white, ultra-modern ferries that link Sardinia with Genoa, Livorno, Piombino and Civitavecchia on the mainland. And this is the essence of Olbia; it is a place that people pass through rather than pass time in, it is above all else a gateway to and from Sardinia.

But our abiding memory of our time here (apart from feline faeces) was eating in a particular restaurant, the one we went to on our second evening and every evening thereafter, the one that Monica said was *particolare*. How right she was.

Monica's recommendation, Li Sciappeddi, was a very

special *agriturismo**. It was about ten kilometres away and somewhere we would just never have found on our own. Yes, it was off the beaten track but at least this time there was a track.

At Li Sciappeddi** there was no menu and no wine list. Each table was already set with red and white wine and water. No bookings were taken after six and the eating experience began between half seven and eight; it reached its hiatus around ten and finished close to eleven. Everyone was encouraged to arrive on time as the highlight, the *porchetta,* the suckling pig, was served to every table at the same time.

So, as we worked our way though all the other courses – and, this being Italy, there were quite a few of those – the wonderful smells of the roasting *porchetta* wafted out from the kitchen. By the time it was cooked, everyone was champing at the bit and every night it was well worth the wait. As was *il conto* – it was a fixed price, at the time, the equivalent of £18 for the two of us!

Porchetta is a Sardinian speciality. Traditionally a large pit was dug in the ground and covered with stones and a fire built on top; after a few hours the young pig was placed on this and covered with hot embers, myrtle branches and finally earth ... my suspicion is that at Li Sciappeddi they didn't go the whole hog. But, what the hell, it didn't seem to matter whether or not they stuck to the traditional recipe, the end result was what counted and each night, although the build-up of courses was mouth-wateringly different, the climax was

---

Agriturismo is holiday accommodation in restored or adapted farmhouses. In Italy the *agriturismo* will normally serve foods and wines prepared and produced on the farm or at least locally. Some, like Li Sciappeddi, also serve as a restaurant for locals and non-resident visitors and, despite their rural settings, many *agriturismi* have first-class accommodation and some even have swimming pools.

**The name Li Sciappeddi refers to the small pieces of wood left over when logs are split with a hatchet or axe.

The looming presence of Isola di Tavolara

the same: succulent, juicy-pink roasted *porchetta* with crispy crackling and fresh uncooked *finocchio*, fennel, on a simple wooden platter followed by a glass of *mirto*, a traditional Sardinian *liquore* made from myrtle berries and leaves.

I had read about another Sardinian speciality, native to the Nuoro region, and literally created around a suckling pig. Called *toro del ciabattino,* it was a suckling pig stuffed inside a wild goat which was inside a calf; and inside the suckling pig was a hare with a partridge inside it and another smaller bird inside the partridge. The name literally means 'the cobbler's bull' and came about because it required the skills of the local cobbler, armed with a needle and strong thread, to sew each ingredient into the one before. It was, I suppose, a sort of gastronomic Russian doll.

Back at Monica's, the cat problem persisted. In an effort to help her find a solution we came up with some suggestions but she had tried them all ... except squirting lemon juice everywhere which, we had heard, was not something cats appreciated. We guessed, from the cats' point of view, the problem was territorial, there being so many of them. But although it was an inconvenience, particularly to the nostrils, this house was still a good place to be.

In her own inimitable way Monica looked after us; during the day she was a tour guide and in her own time she was an accomplished artist, eccentric hostess and carer of cats. All of the time she was both helpful and generous. We never saw her the morning we left but we had had a goodbye drink with her the night before. With clever footwork we packed the car – no cats got in and no soles were soiled. We were on our way back to Scano and the politics of staying with Nuncia and being with Rina.

South of Olbia I was back in Lawrence mode and ready for another round of comparing and contrasting, albeit in reverse as we were travelling south and he had been coming up *from* the south.

Off the east coast of Sardinia, just south of Olbia, is the island of Tavolara. On the map it doesn't look anything special, no more than a long-nailed finger pointing towards the mainland. But Lawrence saw it up close and personal, 'Ahead we saw the big hump of the island of Tavolara, a magnificent mass of rock which fascinated me by its splendid, weighty form.'

From whichever point of the compass you first see Tavolara it dominates the landscape as the coastal plain is relatively flat and most of the island is around 550 metres above sea level. What Lawrence may not have known was that this was probably the world's smallest kingdom and had never been a part of Sardinia; for a time, between 1886 and 1895 it was a republic before the Bertoleoni family was reinstated as the royal line. In theory the Bertoleonis retain that status and Tonino Bertoleoni, who in the summer runs a restaurant on the island, is in reality King Carlo II of Tavolara. Google it and you come up with 'The Kingdom of Tavolara'.

Today Tavolara is a peculiar mix: it is part of Italy although it has never been formally annexed; half the population and most of the sheep were displaced in 1962 when the eastern half became a NATO base; since the late nineties the rest of the island and its surrounding waters have been part of a marine reserve which has restricted tourist facilities. What hasn't changed is how this limestone massif is an ever-present companion to every traveller between Olbia and Nuoro; nobody who comes this way will ever forget the many countenances of this stunning hump of rock.

We pressed on. Tavolara was behind us and we passed the hilltop town of Posada with the 20-metre high ruins of a 12th century fortress dominating the hill on the seaward side. Next stop Siniscola.

In the 1920s the bus from Nuoro to Terranova stopped here for a lunch break; when Lawrence made the trip everyone on board was tired and hungry and eagerly awaiting respite as much from each other as the heat ... 'and there it is, a grey huddle of a village with two towers ... just a narrow crude, stony place, hot in the sun cold in the shade ... the inn did not look promising ... the usual cold room opening gloomily on the gloomy street ... the usual long table ... with a foully blotched tablecloth'.

Lawrence's description of eating in Siniscola should be read by everyone who has ever had an altercation at a restaurant – it might just put things in perspective.

So, there we were, less demanding than the irksome Lawrence, but nevertheless seeking somewhere to re-energise in Siniscola. As ever we headed for the cluster of old men and sat with them outside in the sun and downed a beer. Sometimes it's hard to tell the age of the elderly Italian male but I guessed that maybe one or two hereabouts might be in their nineties. And, if so, then one of these venerable citizens of Siniscola, as a seven- or eight-year old, might have played in these very streets the day Lawrence and the queen bee stopped by for a bite to eat. Perhaps one of them had an older sister or a mother who was the waitress here, the one Lawrence called the 'sludge queen'. Lawrence marked their card but they probably never gave him a second glance.

It wasn't far to Nuoro which Lawrence knew to be the birthplace of the Sardinian writer Grazia Deledda*, who went on to win the Nobel Prize for Literature in 1926. So, initially, he was kindly disposed to the place; he also happened upon a

---

*Ironically a number of years later Lawrence was asked to provide the Introduction to the English translation of Deledda's La Madre, The Mother. Curiously he never mentioned that he had ever been in Sardinia nor that he had passed through her home town of Nuoro.

masked carnival procession which he appeared to enjoy and gave him much to write about but, when the time came to leave, he was less than affectionate about the local culture, 'there is nothing to see in Nuoro: which, to tell the truth, is always a relief.'

Lawrence stayed overnight in Nuoro but this time we by-passed it and headed due west towards Macomér and Scano and that was the last we heard from our unseen companion. For us his journey between Nuoro and Terranova had been both fascinating and entertaining ... I wondered whether one day I might rejoin him on his journey from Taormina in Sicily to Cagliari, Nuoro and beyond.

All change at Scano

We were on familiar territory; as we traversed Sardinia's central plain we were working on a strategy for our first few hours in Scano. We decided we should see Rina first before heading to Nuncia's to eat and settle in for the night. Only problem was I'd forgotten the bit of paper with Rina's telephone number and address.

There are some new houses on the outskirts of Scano and on our last visit Rina had mentioned that her brother lived next door to the one with the pink door. Well, it was a start.

We didn't know which side 'next door' was but a toss of a coin later I knocked the door on the right and asked if Rina's brother lived there. He did and his daughter directed me down to his den, the garage, from where he called Rina. Five minutes later and that familiar battered Fiat Uno shot round the corner, came to a frenetic halt and deposited a joyous Rina at our feet.

Reunions can sometimes be a disappointment but not this one. It began in the street with all the usual kissing and hugging and exchange of presents and ended almost three hours later when we finally left Rina's house en route to Nuncia's.

We had followed Rina home and were made very welcome

by both her parents. Her father was older than his brother Pietro but, unlike Pietro, he did have a state-of-the-art-all-singing-and-dancing black leather armchair and he proudly demonstrated how it turned, lifted, rocked and extended. Now, I'm not one to be taken in by the latest gadget, but it *was* very impressive, the more so because it wasn't what I expected to find in Scano, particularly as I knew that Rina's father still spent much of his day outdoors tending his vines. It seemed somehow incongruous, a bit like finding the wonderful Dory Perria in Cuglieri six months earlier.

Rina's mother, a bubbly fifty-something with a twinkle in her eye, had definitely worn a lot better than many Italian women of the same age. My guess is that it was that twinkle. Before we'd even got as far as the house we could see she was a keen gardener and, despite the restrictions of language, she and Kay had already exchanged notes on all sorts of gardening gossip that was way beyond me even in English.

Once inside, and after the chair demo, we sat and talked, looked at photos, nibbled a bit of this, drank a little of that ... until, that is, I mentioned the golden elixir. You see, all along we had thought that this was something that Rina's mother had bought ... we didn't realise that she had made it ... nor that she had only one bottle left. Despite our feeble protestations she insisted that we share it but not before we sat her under a bright light and extracted the recipe.

It was very simple.

For three litres you need the following:

A 3-litre Kilner-type jar with a wide neck

2 oranges

80 coffee beans

Grappa (around 2.5 litres)

Between 800gm and 1kilo sugar (depending on how sweet you like your liquor)

And this is what you do:

· With a sharp knife make forty cuts into the skin of each orange and push a coffee bean into each cut

· Pour about half the grappa into the jar, add the sugar and shake (with the top on) till the sugar is almost dissolved

· Carefully add the bean-impregnated oranges and top up with grappa; seal and give a good shake

· Store in a cool, cupboard for forty days, gently shaking every few days to make sure all the sugar is dissolved

· Bottle and drink

Forty, as you will have noticed, is a recurring theme in this recipe so there's probably some religious significance in its origins – but, trust me, 38 days and 42 days work just as well! Also, not surprisingly, by far the best place to buy the *grappa* is Italy where it's about one third of the price.

So, clutching half a bottle of the ready-made stuff and the 'secret' recipe wandering around the memory cells, we said our interim goodbyes to Rina and her family and headed across town to Nuncia's. We knew we'd see them all again before we left.

What a difference six months makes.

We arrived at Nuncia's at eight to the usual round of greetings ... by now we were getting the hang of the double kiss and were looking less surprised when the second kiss sneaked up behind the first. Nuncia and Pietro were delighted to see us – as, indeed, we were them – and showed us to our room and told us to come through to the dining room when we were ready.

In the dining room, busier than usual, a less chirpy Nuncia was waiting for us at our usual table. Things had changed here, we could see that, and we could sense that Nuncia didn't embrace the changes. For a start there were menus on all the tables but they were not for Nuncia's creative cuisine, they were for pizzas; and, of course, Nuncia was on the customer side of the serving hatch and her son, Ricardo was in charge of the pizza-making.

We could see that Nuncia did not like this turn of events but she realised that, as and when Ricardo was ready to take over the business, then he had to do things his way, the modern way and the young people of Scano clearly couldn't get enough of his pizzas. It was the 21st century and Nuncia was not one to fly in the face of progress, though there was no reason why she couldn't go along with things *and* grit her teeth at the same time.

Almost embarrassed she passed us the menu and asked us to choose our pizza ... and, no, she didn't follow up with, 'Hi, I'm Nuncia and I'll be your personal waitress this evening'.

I have to say, give Ricardo his due, it was a bloody good pizza, and I'm not the world's biggest pizza fan.

So, while we were firmly focused on the Scano of six months ago, things on the ground had moved on and, like it or not, take-away pizzas were literally the order of the day.

Yes, we were disappointed that things had changed but more for Nuncia than for ourselves and, whether or not she picked up on this I can't be certain but, whatever the reason, Nuncia decided to rebel. For the next three evenings she invented a loophole in the arrangement with Ricardo which stated that her paying guests would be fed by her and her alone or else there'd be trouble. The Independent Republic of Nuncia was born and the *status quo* was restored – while all around us could be heard the chomping of pizzas, across an imaginary border in our corner of the dining room things were as they had always been.

The twinkle had returned to Nuncia's eye.

As we'd already done a fair bit of motoring we decided not to venture too far from Scano for the next three days and, besides, we'd come here to spend time with our friends and to relax.

So if we weren't at Nuncia's or with Rina and her parents, we were at 'our' Nuraghe, where restoration seemed to have come to an abrupt halt, or at Bosa or Macomér, the two largest towns within a half-hour drive.

We had been to Bosa many times but could never resist returning to sample its charms and walk under the palms alongside the Temo, Sardinia's only navigable river, or climb the narrow winding *vicoli* of the mediæval quarter of Sa Costa up to the Castello Malaspina. It's one of those places that wherever you turn there is something to see, someone to chat to, somewhere to explore ... and the shops are good too, provided you get there early (or late) enough.

As Rina couldn't eat with us in the evening, we brought her here instead for lunch and afterwards introduced her to our favourite local source of *gelato*, ice-cream, that we'd sussed out on our first ever day in Sardinia.

We drove back alongside the Temo to the small coastal resort of Bosa Marina with its fine beach and crescent-shaped harbour. This was the second time we'd come across an inland town with an offshoot on the coast – Marina di Orosei near the Grotta di Ispinigoli is three kilometres from inland Orosei. This phenomenon can be seen throughout Italy and appears to have its origins in a younger generation realising the potential of their nearby coastline and emigrating the few kilometres to the sea to establish a new settlement.

Macomér, on the other hand, was initially just a town we skirted round on the road to somewhere else, we'd never actually ventured up the hill and into the town. But, according to Rina, this was the main town in the area, the place people went to get anything and everything they couldn't buy in Scano or on market day.

I was checking out the route on the map when something struck me about Macomér, it was at the crossroads of modern Sardinia's road and rail network. When we went to Sassari we returned to Scano via Macomér; when we went to and from Cagliari we went via Macomér; and when we went to and from Nuoro we went via Macomér. North-south it's bang in the middle; east-west it's towards the western end of Sardinia's waist, with Nuoro at the eastern end. Quite simply, there's nowhere of any size in the central plain, possibly because, until the 1950s, this area in particular was rampant with malaria* – I also recall Lawrence making reference to this low-lying problem.

Initially Macomér just seemed like any other small Italian town not on any tourist trail: a little bit run-down, in need of a few more shops and a few more litter bins. We had been wandering round for about an hour and only managed to buy one thing, a quirky mouse-mat for the thirteen year-old son of a friend until, that is, we happened upon Il Buon Gustaio, literally good taste, a delicatessen, specialising in local *formaggi*, cheeses, and cold meats.

Here was a veritable gem. Here you could taste and buy the best that Sardinia has to offer, the wonderful Pecorino Sardo made from the milk of local sheep (which Sardinians maintain is the most sought-after Pecorino on the mainland) and Dolci di Macomér, a traditional mild cheese made from cows' milk. As well as cheeses, the Macomér area specialises in *salsicce* (sausages) and *salami* and at Il Buon Gustaio they had the lot and showed it off like works of art.

The only problem was that all we could do was look,

*In his introduction to *South to Sardinia*, Alan Ross describes Sardinia as an island, 'stewing in its malarial fevers'. But in the 1950s things improved and he was able to report that: 'The last few years have seen a complete change. Largely through American financial aid and research, malaria – which the Sards call *intemperie* … has been completely cleared. Marshes have been drained, the hills reforested, and every house bears its DDT spray-date'.

point, admire, inhale and salivate and, of course, graciously accept the free samples as and when offered ... but we couldn't buy because Nuncia was feeding us back in Scano and we couldn't really import these fresh foods into the UK.

*

It's my hair that does it every time. It used to be reddish-fair but now it was almost white and I think that's why whenever we're in Italy I'm invariably asked in German, "*Deutscher?*" The thing is my German is better than my Italian so I regularly confuse such interrogators a little further by replying *in German*, denying that I am German, "*Nein, Ich bin aus Irland.*" Saying I'm from Ireland, in German, causes further confusion. It's a game I enjoy.

So, when we were eating at Nuncia's one evening, I was not entirely surprised when a young woman at the next table said to me in Italian, "*E tedesco?*" Yet again I was being asked if I was German. So, I churned out my stock response, "*Nein, Ich bin aus Irland.*" Initially this threw her ... she'd spoken in Italian, I'd replied in German saying that I was not German but, in effect, English-speaking. She recovered quickly and laughed; she got the joke.

Renata was German, her partner, Roberto, was from Scano but had lived in Germany (where they met) but now both had moved to Sardinia and bought an old farmhouse with a piece of land close to Scano. We chatted in ital-germ-glish as gradually our two tables became one.

Renato was dark, winsome and determined; Roberto, also dark but tall for an Italian, had that confident air that comes from having lived abroad and returned home; both were earnest and enterprising. They wanted to live off the land and exuded confidence and enthusiasm as they shared their goals with two complete strangers. They also knew how to enjoy themselves so there was an increase in the *liquori* count that evening and a fair amount of raucous laughter, in ital-germ-glish of course.

Renato and Roberto came in for a drink the next evening while we were eating and came over to ask us if we'd like to come to the farm the following morning and collect some wild asparagus in the woods. Roberto would meet us outside Nuncia's, we'd follow him to the farm then he'd go off to do some work on another farm and Renata would show us round. We thought about it for a nano-second and, weather-permitting arranged to meet at ten.

Rain was in the air as Roberto swung open the gate to their farm. Rather than following the well-worn track, he cut up through an oak copse to the right which he said was quicker … it was also steeper and he was a good twenty-five years younger but we kept up and it probably did us good. When we could see Renato at the top where the trees thinned out Roberta turned, pointed to her, "*lassù*", he said and raced back down the hill to his pick-up, waving goodbye as he did so. We carried on up and joined Renata on the level land where the farmhouse stood.

It was a low stone structure, sturdy enough but with a paucity of roofs and an assortment of add-ons that looked like they had outstayed their welcome. We had the grand tour, inside and out, and knew that our assessment of their determination and enthusiasm had been spot on. Lack of money was forcing them to take their time but slow progress meant that what they did do was of the highest quality. Yes, not every room had the advantage of a roof, but they lived in the ones that did in the knowledge that one day they'd get there. In some of the outhouses there were pigs and chickens and, in the fields beyond, a few cattle.

It was clearly a haphazard existence, they weren't yet living off the land but they had some savings and helped out on other farms to earn a bit extra. They were growing vegetables and sometimes had some over to sell. And the woods supplied them free of charge, with wild asparagus, *asparagi selvatici*), which was, after all, why we were there.

Renata confessed she'd picked a lot the day before so we might not find many – she was right but in our case it was because we didn't know what we were looking for – but once Renata found the first we were on a roll. A sort of slow-motion roll for, truth be told, there was just enough for a couple of helpings which Renato insisted we pass on to Nuncia … who dutifully passed them back to us as part of our evening meal. Unknown to us at the time, that lesson in harvesting wild asparagus was to serve us well in the future … but that, as they say, is *un'altra storia*.

It had been an exhilarating and even humbling experience to spend those few hours with Renata. As the rain started the three of us took the more serpentine track down to the gate where we thanked Renata for allowing us to share her passion and her asparagus; we wished her and Roberto well – we knew we wouldn't see them again this holiday for the next day we would be heading back to Alghero.

We had our last breakfast in Scano sitting out in the sun but the brightness and warmth of the day couldn't hide the sense of sadness as we prepared again for the inevitable round of thank-yous and goodbyes. Kay and I are not good at these and neither are most Italians … we both prolong that final back-turning moment when eyes no longer meet and the reality of the parting takes over.

Nuncia, on the other hand, is from Iscia and she just got on with it and made it easy all-round. As we pulled away from the bar and waved out the car windows we weren't sure if we'd be back this way but we knew that if and when we were, we'd be made very welcome.

Ten minutes later we were doing it all again on the Rina side of town. Her mother gave us some fruit for the journey and some jars and bottles for the larder back home but sadly her father's routine was not to be broken and he had pottered off to tend his vines. And quite right too ... it also meant that I got to sit in his chair and play with the buttons!

As we headed out of Scano we had mixed feelings. Although it was unspoken, I think we both knew that we'd not be back this way in the immediate future but that nonetheless it was a place with which we had a special attachment. There were people here we could call friends, people who had touched our lives and whose lives we had touched in turn. It was a place that few English-speaking visitors had even passed through; and it's a place that the young will always leave and perhaps, like Roberto, return to with new perspectives. And it's a place that we will return to if only to see who makes the best orange and coffee *liquore*.

With such thoughts wandering round our heads, we decided to return to Alghero the back way, to the east of the mountains, and give the coast road a miss. It would give *us* a new perspective and there was a slim chance that we might sight the rare griffin vulture that still nests in this part of Sardinia.

The vulture eluded us but, as compensation, we had magnificent views of Alghero as the road wound down out of the mountains and back onto the coastal plain. In the distance we could see the glint of aircraft taking off and landing at the airport.

The following morning we were on one.

The other side of Sicily

I let out an audible 'Yes!'. I'd just read the latest 'New Routes' email from Ryanair and discovered that, at long last, they were going to fly to Palermo in Sicily. A few clicks later and I'd booked our flights; destination Palermo ... what happened after that we still had to organise.

After much map-browsing we decided to explore the south and west of the island and leave a return to Siracusa and the Teatro Greco for another time. Within a few days everything was sorted: we'd fly on the early morning flight to Palermo, head down the coast to Castellammare del Golfo for a night before cutting across to the south coast to our main destination, Sciacca, for nine days and then another day in Castellammare del Golfo on the way back to Palermo and home.

Of course it's the western side of Sicily that has the bad reputation in relation to *La Cosa Nostra*. On some maps (including mine) the airport serving Palermo is still called Punta Raisi and while Punta Raisi remains its location, its name had been changed to Falcone e Borsellino in memory of the two magistrates who were murdered by the mafia in 1992.

Tyrrhenian
Sea

Punto Raisi

Capo San Vito

Palermo

Erice

**CASTELLAMMARE
DEL GOLFO**

Trápani

Segesta

Gibellina Nuova

Marsala

Gibellina *(ruins)*

SICILY

Enna

Menfi

Caltabellotta

SCIACCA

Eraclea Minoa

Agrigento

Palermo to Trápani · 110km

As we approached the airport I was re-reading Peter Robb's *Midnight in Sicily* and thinking about these two men, Giovanni Falcone and Paolo Borsellino, who tried to bring the mafia to heel and ended up with their names on an airport.

The first to die was Falcone, blown up with his wife and three escorts on the road linking Palermo with Punta Raisi. In Italy it was one of those events, a bit like the fall of Margaret Thatcher in England or the fall of New York's Twin Towers, when people remember where they were and what they were doing at the time. It stopped Italy in its tracks and was the beginning of the end of the 'heroic' mafia myth. Two months later his colleague Borsellino was killed with five of his escorts by another bomb planted outside his mother's house. Battle was engaged and, if nothing else, nobody now could deny the existence of the mafia.

When we landed it was drizzling so we changed our plans for the day. It had only just gone ten in the morning and we had planned to do a bit of sightseeing, perhaps head for Palermo or the Greek temple at Segesta before checking in at Residence Aziyz later in the afternoon. But we decided instead to go straight to Castellammare del Golfo and then, if it cleared up a bit, we could head off somewhere else in the afternoon. We hadn't said what time we would arrive but imagined it wouldn't be a problem.

We arrived in Castellammare del Golfo shortly before midday and checked out the town centre map on the seafront for the Via Guglielmo Marconi. It was clearly marked and in a few minutes we were there. There was one parking space about a dozen metres from the Residence Aziyz sign; we pulled in.

The street was deserted but for three people: one, a woman in her mid-fifties, stood in the entrance to our hotel; another, a younger man in his late-twenties, stood on the pavement between us and the woman; the third, a man in his early-sixties, was on the other side of the street opposite the woman. They were clearly looking for someone or something but, when we pulled up, their attention began to focus on us.

Slowly we got out of the car. They were clearly watching us but trying (and failing) to be nonchalent about it. We could 'do' nonchalant too and chatted casually as we walked to the boot of the car and raised it. Still no obvious reaction other than the straining of a neck or three. It wasn't till I took the first bag out of the boot and set it on the pavement that they struck.

Almost before we realised it, the two men had left their posts and had made a bee-line for the back of the car … and, having confirmed that we were indeed heading for the Residence Aziyz, insisted on carrying our bags into the hotel where the woman was waiting to greet us.

It wasn't till we settled into our room and had a chance to catch our breath that all was made clear … we were their first ever guests and they'd been waiting for us *all* day. Little did they know that, but for the drizzle, they would have had another five hours to wait!

Residence Aziyz was an old renovated mansion and the whole family, mother, father and two sons, had worked hard to reach this point. Being the first guests, we were expected to inspect the works from top to bottom, and to register our approval. This we did in the interests of diplomatic relations between our two great countries (in my case that was Italy and Ireland) and we most definitely approved. It was truly magnificent … what they hadn't spent on air-conditioning, they'd spent on marble and simple and stylish decor; on the Residence Ayziz website this was understated as 'utmost care and attention'.

In a nutshell, we were honoured to be their first guests and when we returned from an evening meal overlooking the harbour we sat with the family in their open-air courtyard surrounded by two dictionaries, one Italian-English, the other English-Italian, well into the wee small hours helping make their dream come true.

For the record, when we came back this way just over a week later, we were also their second guests ... and were honoured to be so; their third guest was an American woman, three days later.

The next morning we set off for Verdetecnica, an old Sicilian farmhouse converted to self-catering units on the western side of Monte Kronio, the mountain that oversees the coastal fishing port of Sciacca (pronounced *shaka*).

Verdetecnica was run by Salvatore, a Sicilian, and his French wife Pascale and, surprise, surprise, they both spoke near-perfect English. As well as offering accommodation, the site housed a small nursery run by Salvatore to supply his garden design business.

We seemed to have done it again, our 'unit' was just the right balance of exposed beams and mod cons and the whole setting was stunning. But Verdetechnica was the sum of its parts and the two most important 'parts' here were the jaunty Salvatore and the gentle Pascale. Always there, always helpful, always open.

It wasn't long before Salvatore and I realised we had something in common. I was eyeing up the library behind the reception area and spotted a copy of *Midnight in Sicily* in English and mentioned the book to Salvatore who immediately became animated.

'You've read it?' he asked as if he'd found a soul-mate.

'Yes, and I'm reading it again, I've got it with me. Did *you* read it in English?

Salvatore shrugged his shoulders, 'I had to ... it's not published in Italian.'

'Why not?'

He shrugged his shoulders again, 'Italians don't want to hear some of these things.'

I understood what he was saying and it was a subject we returned to from time to time, particularly when he heard that we'd just come from Castellammare del Golfo.

On our one afternoon in Castellammare del Golfo we'd wandered round the town and it all seemed quite normal ... castle, beach, restaurants, shops (closed!); on our way to the harbour in the evening we discovered the old tuna fishery, all that was left of the industry once based here; the harbour itself was picturesque and we ate well in a restaurant overlooking the sea. No men in dark suits and dark glasses, no severed horse's head, no-one burning copies of *Midnight in Sicily* ... nothing at all untoward.

The thought that this little place might have had any part to play in mafia mythology never crossed our minds. Little it might have been but it gave its name to one of the most famous of the 'mafia' wars in prohibition America – the Castellammarese war of 1930-31 which involved a faction led by Salvatore Maranzano who hailed from this corner of south-west Sicily. Brooklyn-based 'Joe Bananas' and members of the notorious Magaddinos family could also claim Castellammare del Golfo as their 'home'.*

It has been said that, at the height of internecine feuding in the 1950s in Castellammare del Golfo itself, some eighty percent of the adult male population had been in prison and

*Although many of the Sicilian mafia immigrated to America, many of those that became notorious, particularly during the prohibition era, were either born in America or grew up there. And, of course, not all the American mafia were Sicilian – the most notorious of them all, Al Capone, was born in America of Neapolitan parents.

some sixty percent are said to have been involved in at least one killing. That said, I'm not exactly sure how the latter statistic was arrived at as a door-to-door survey doesn't seem likely. On our return to the Residence Aziyz maybe we'd view this place in a slightly different light.

Back in Sciacca all was well with the world. We had found a place to eat, Santa Lucia, about a kilometre further up Monte Kronia, and we knew almost immediately that this was the place for us, not only because it was frequented almost exclusively by locals but also because of the quality of the food. On reflection, perhaps one is a prerequisite of the other.

It was run by another husband-and-wife team, Francesca was the waitress and Carlo the chef and it was while eating here that I first started to assess restaurants by the quality and variety of their *antipasti*. Every night Carlo and Francesca created an *antipasti* buffet of home-made dishes made with *melanzane, asparagi, zucchini, funghi, peperoni, carciofe, cipolle, cavolfiore, uova, pomodore e proscuitto*. You could choose what and how much you wanted and they were all mouth-watering masterpieces.

The couple had three children, ten-year old Gino, nine-year old Tommaso and seven-year old Maria and the two boys were already doing their bit for the family business. Normally it was Francesca who would take our order but both Gino and Tommaso had been well trained and particularly liked to help out with waiting on us – as soon as we came in they'd have our usual jug of red wine and a couple of glasses on the table in seconds. I think they liked having us around because they could practise their few basic English words and phrases ... and when Maria tried to get in on the act they very quickly shooed her into the adjacent dining area.

On our last night here, a Monday, we were paying the

bill and saying our final goodbyes (we were actually leaving Sciacca on the Wednesday but the restaurant was closed on Tuesdays) when Gino had an animated argument with his mother and father, the gist of which was that he didn't want them to close this particular Tuesday so that we could eat there. I think Francesca considered it but Carlo was clearly weary after a hectic weekend (in which we had also played a part) and needed his rest.

So on the Tuesday we ate at the more up-market, more fashionable, more tourist-orientated Le Gourmet restaurant. Well, if being up-market and fashionable requires that you watch the largest cockroach you've ever seen walk across your tablecloth, then I guess this place was top notch! Equally disturbing was the way in which the waiter whisked it onto the floor, in the vain hope that we'd not actually seen it, and hastily crunched it under foot as if we were deaf as well as blind.

Sciacca was different from Siracusa in that, for us, it was initially a base from which we could explore south-west Italy and less of an attraction in itself. But that changed and once we got to know the town we enjoyed exploring the narrow streets, the cafés and the markets.

There are, in effect, two towns: there's the walled town sited on a broad plateau overlooking the 'other' Sciacca, the port and its attendant community below. And overseeing both is Monte Kronio. It took us some time to work out how to get from one to the other by car, from the walled town down to the port. There were apparently two routes, one on each side of the town, but we only ever found the one.

There was a small daily fruit and vegetable market but the main market was on a Saturday by one of the town's three arched gateways and it was here that I nearly made a huge financial miscalculation in my search for a pair of sandals.

All Italian markets have a large number of shoe stalls and you *can* pick up bargains. I had been hovering around one particular stall wondering whether or not I should splash out on a pair of sandals at €20. I couldn't see my size, normally 41 – there was 40 and there was 42 but no size 41. I asked the guy if he had a 41 but he shook his head, '*Quarantuno, no*'. He tried to get me to try the 40 but I declined. We left the market empty-handed.

About an hour later we were back in the lower end of the town, heading for an *espresso* and a *cappuccino,* when we happened to pass a *negozio di scarpe*, a shoe shop, and there in the window was a pair of sandals identical to the ones in the market, except for the price tag, €17! We went in and I tried on size 41 ... they were too big ... I tried on 40 and they were fine ... I bought them.

As we were leaving, I knew that I'd have to tell the shopkeeper about the pair at the market for €20. I just couldn't resist it. After a few false starts, I managed to get the message across but I wasn't sure whether he appreciated the irony of it or not. He winced rather than smiled.

We had our coffees and headed back to the car. As we walked back past the same shoe shop I glanced in the window; there had been an unexpected burst of inflation in Sciacca, the same pair of sandals, still in his window, was now priced at €20!

The mafia notwithstanding, south-west Sicily is a fascinating place. Five examples: Agrigento, Eraclea Minoa, Gibellina, Marsala and Menfi. Probably only one of these would make it onto the average tourist's itinerary – Agrigento.

On a particularly hot day we 'did' the Valle dei Templi close to Agrigento. We wandered in and out and around the remains of the Temple of Hercules, the Temple of Concord and the Temple of Hera basking in the golden midday sun, looked up to by a meadow of poppies swaying in the gentle breeze. Our camera fingers were working overtime as we tried to do justice to these relics of a Greek civilisation dating from the 6th and 5th centuries BCE. Kay bought a wonderful straw hat here to add to her burgeoning collection ... hopefully sometime she'll remember that if you take one with you, then you won't need to buy another.

It was an extraordinary day. But probably our abiding memory of it was the wrong turning we took before we even got to the *templi* when we ended up in the middle of a livestock market, in Agrigento's shadow, in the middle of nowhere in particular, just there, a seemingly impromptu Sunday get-together of the local agricultural community, mainly men, by the side of the road.

We had to stop and not surprisingly we got some strange looks (perhaps it was the shorts, more likely the white legs) from the many ageing weather-worn faces, eyes still curious, shoulders and hands work-weary, *coppola* (Sicilian cap) firmly fixed at a jaunty angle, teeth an optional extra. The younger generation was there too, more animated, shouting the odds, doing the deals, drawing on cigarettes, waiting for *il telefonino* to ring.

Although there was some farm produce for sale alongside bits and pieces of machinery and tools, this was basically a chance to barter for and buy livestock, much of it sooner or later for the pot. Central to the process was the sharpener of knives, his foot ever treading the trestle to spin the large grinding wheel that would sent everyone home with tools fit for purpose ... killing, cutting up and carving.

This was the sort of haphazard gathering that would not happen in the UK because of issues around possible maltreatment of animals or health and safety regulations. But we did not see any animals being maltreated, other than being the focus of attention as an 'item' for sale or to be bargained over. Kay and I kept chickens, probably the most mollycoddled chickens in the universe, and we have seen how chickens are sometimes kept in Italy and, yes, it's not always up to our back-garden-in-rural-England standards but still infinitely better than the life inflicted on the average supermarket, non free-range, bird.

The basic difference here was that people were buying their *secundo piatto* while it was still alive and kicking, they were cutting out the middle man, the *supermercato*. In the case of the chickens, it meant that two or three defiantly squawking birds were put into a cardboard box peppered with air holes (the box, not the chickens), taken home and despatched as required.

As well as *galline* (chickens) there were *cavalli* (horses), *puledri* (foals), *maiali* (pigs), *bestiame* (cattle) and *pecori* (sheep) and although the horses may well have had a few years work left in them, they were just as likely to have been for the pot; in some parts of Italy, particularly Apulia and Sardinia, *cavallo* is often on the menu, very occasionally the only meat on the menu.

We would have had liked to photograph this place and these people going about their Sunday business but had deliberately left our cameras in the car; in a sense we were intruders and it did not seem appropriate to turn the normality of the occasion into a curiosity.

After we left the *templi* we headed for the sprawling, untidy hillside mass that was Agrigento itself. On the lower slopes we happened upon a busy *pasticceria* that sold the most wonderful pastries we had ever seen and indulged ourselves as we watched the world go by. But this was as far as we got. Unusually for us, this was a place where we didn't feel comfortable; there was no logic to it, perhaps it was the contrast with the 'other' Agrigento, the *templi*. Back on the main road we looked up at the town and thought how lucky we were to be staying in Sciacca.*

On another day we again headed east from Sciacca to Eraclea Minoa, little more than a small dot on the map halfway to Agrigento. Originally the site of an ancient Mycenean settlement, the 6th century BCE Spartan site is perched on the edge of a cliff overlooking the sea, one end of the pine-edged white sands of the sweeping Capo Bianco.

What was remarkable about this place (apart from the fact that, for most of the time, we were the only two people there) was that not only could you 'see' the city clearly from its foundations but you could bend down and pick it up. Bits of pottery, for example, were just lying on the ground; if we had been so inclined, we could have just put a few pieces in our pockets. Needless to say, we didn't but it added to the atmosphere in that we felt as if we were discovering something and touching artefacts that had been undisturbed for thousands of years.

The site boasts a theatre which, having been constructed of a soft, friable stone, lies under a protective plastic canopy. Yes, it spoils the effect but, if it is a compromise between being accessible and being preserved, then why not? As with most Greek theatres it looks out to sea, a stunning backcloth to every performance.

---

*In his book *The Dark Heart of Italy*, Tobias Jones sheds some light on the other side to Agrigento which was known as the *zoccolo duro*, the mafia's 'hard hoof'. Writing in 2002, he described the local phenomenon of *abusivismo*, illegal building, 'not chaotic lawlessness but precision profiteering', that was out of control in and around Agrigento and which the authorities were cracking down on. Jones was in Agrigento the week the bulldozing was supposed to begin but it never did ... a new Prime Minister had just been elected, one Silvio Berlusconi, the first in history to have secured all sixty-one Sicilian parliamentary seats!

Gibellina has a past too. It lies north-west of Sciacca in the Valle del Belice and was the largest of three towns devastated by an earthquake in 1968 – the other two were Poggioreale and Salaparuta. On the map there are now two of each: the new town of Gibellina and the *Ruderi di* Gibellina, the ruins of Gibellina.

The ruins of Poggioreale and Salaparuta are just that, the decaying ruins of two forgotten hillside villages but Gibellina is different. In 1989 the artist Alberto Burri created an artwork, *Cretto* (Crack), out of what was left of Gibellina, a stark and controversial memorial to a tragedy still in the public memory.

When we saw it for the first time it took our breath away. In one sense we knew what to expect, the ruins of the town covered in concrete, but with the streets and alleyways remaining crack-like in a white landscape. We rounded a bend on the winding road and there it was, the white concrete shimmering in the sunlight. But only the main part of the town was concreted over, there remained a scattering of houses on the outskirts that still stood, sentinel-like, watching our every move. These abandoned shells, their ragged and faded curtains fluttering through glassless windows in the warm breeze, were all that remained of the humanity that once lived and loved here.

We were the only visitors to Gibellina that morning. We walked the streets together, and separately, as the small *lucertole* (lizards), disturbed by our presence, scurried away into their modern concrete homes. Controversial it might have been, but it had both a starkness and a curiously compelling beauty. Above all there was the silence, an almost unbearable silence.

Eventually the people of Gibellina were rehoused in Gibellina Nuova, close to the *autostrada* eighteen kilometres away, but not before corrupt politicians and the mafia had

The concrete streets of Gibellina

hijacked the monies set aside for the initial reconstruction.*
We drove to the new town and, despite the efforts made to
pepper it with countless artworks, found it to be a desolate,
uninspiring place seemingly devoid of people. The streets
were wide and straight and it was easy to park, not at all like
the Italy we knew and loved.

Now Marsala, that's an altogether different proposition. I'm
ashamed to say that I underestimated the time it would take
to get there and, yes, we did it again, we arrived just fifteen
minutes before the beginning of the end ... of shopping that is.

But we were in defiant mode and got to what we thought
was the place to buy Marsala itself ... sadly it was the Marsala
museum where we could find out all about the renowned
liquor but not actually purchase any. That became apparent
when I asked for a bottle of that stuff behind the glass case,
please ... the museum curator was adamant but helpful. She
said the place we wanted, Morsi & Sorsi, was about two
hundred metres down the road and they closed in less than
five minutes. We decided to make a run for it while the nice
curator gave them a ring and said we were on our way and
that we were loaded with cash.

Breathless we fell into the store while are around it was the
shuttered silence of the *siesta*. The message had got through
... we were expected ... the glasses were ready ... battle was
joined.

The shop was now shut and for the first time we were
on the inside! Our genial host smiled his way through the
grand tour and the history of Marsala (and its strong English

---

*I later discovered that a close friend had been in Sicily at the time of the
earthquake and got involved in the humanitarian relief effort in Gibellina and
the other two towns. He painted a picture of organised chaos with many
unrecovered bodies remaining under the rubble; some, it was said later, were
there so long they were eaten by domestic pigs.

connections*) and deftly confused us with the special nuances of this one and that one, the differences between the *Fine*, *Superiore* and the *Vergine***. We tasted and agreed. The more he explained, the more we agreed, the more we tasted.

An hour later we knew we liked them all and, clutching our purchases and in desperate need of food, we fell out of Morci & Sorci into the sunlight and what was left of the siesta.

We returned to Marsala several times, not solely for the Morci & Sorci experience, though we always popped in to pay our respects, it was the decent thing to do, but because we really liked the feel of the place. After Siracusa comes Marsala.

Menfi was a place we always by-passed. The main road, the *superstrada*, to the north of the town was closed – there had been a minor quaking of the earth about six months earlier and the powers-that-be were still inspecting the tall concrete stilts that carry it across the valley. The signposted diversion was a very long way round so, with the help of Salvatore, we found an alternative way west which took us just south of Menfi.

It wasn't that we were deliberately trying to avoid the place, there was just no need to go there; it was the place between the soon-to-be-inspected road and the short cut.

---

*The Marsala fortified wines were brought to a wider market in the late 18th century after the English trader, John Woodhouse landed at the town and realised that the wines here were a good substitute for Portuguese port and Spanish sherry. He returned to Marsala and set up a business and was later joined by another Englishman, Ben Ingham. In the late 19th century Woodhouse and Ingham were bought up by a Sicilian company, Florio, now all part of the Cinzano group.

**Although there are some variations, the five basic Marsala wines are as follows: *Marsala Fine* (matured for one year); *Superiore* (matured for two years); *Superiore Riserva* (matured for four years); *Vergine* (matured for five years); *Vergine Riserva* (matured for ten years). As I write, I am enjoying a glass of the latter, *oltre 10 anni d'invecchiamento*, matured for more than ten years.

Truth be told, we've never actually been there ... well not physically anyway.

All the main UK supermarket chains sell at least one Sicilian red wine but they are not all the same. Some, by far the best ones, originate in the Menfi area. Any wine from Menfi or *Inycon* (they are one and the same) is generally worth more than a second slurp. Sadly we did not know what we were missing by not getting lost and stumbling upon Menfi. We'll not make that mistake again and next time we'll try to be around in the first week in July for the annual wine festival, *Inycon–Menfi e il suo vino*.

We left Verdetecnica early in the morning for we wanted to get to Marsala and on to Trápani, Erice and, if possible, San Vito lo Capo before we hit (an unfortunate choice of word bearing in mind what we now know) Castellammare del Golfo around five in the afternoon. We asked Salvatore if he would call Residence Aziyz and tell them what time to expect us – the last thing we wanted was the whole family cluttering up the streets most of the day in fruitless, though understandable, anticipation

At Marsala we had time to indulge in a couple of hours of retail therapy before heading north towards Trápani and Erice ... and instead by-passed both to head cross-country to San Vito lo Capo at the northern-most tip of the Reserva Naturale della Zingaro, a 4000-acre nature reserve.

We would have done better to spend the rest of the afternoon in Zingaro Reserve but the thought of missing 'the northern-most tip' of anywhere was out of the question so we went for it. It was dramatic, it was hot, the limpid aquamarine sea was beautiful and the beach was probably beautiful too ... except that, being covered in bodies, you couldn't actually see it.

San Vito lo Capo was a modern holiday resort, the sort of

place that suits many people, particularly families with young children, but that we instinctively avoided. Still, we'd made it this far so we did what we always do in such situations, we look for the best source of *gelati*, ice-creams. It wasn't difficult to find somewhere and we sat in the shade to enjoy our treat when we were joined by the English family-on-holiday from hell.

The worst thing was that we had clocked this same family before, they had been on our flight from Stansted and, when we landed at Palermo, we were more than a little relieved to know that we'd never clap eyes on them again. But here they were, stalking us in a café in San Vito lo Capo ... running round, shouting, knocking things over, swearing ... and the children were just as bad! Worse was still to come; we overheard (it wasn't difficult) their plans for the next day ... they were catching the same flight as us back to London.

Time for us to go and get a head start. We shot out of San Vito lo Capo and headed back south and east – the erstwhile mafia stronghold of Castellammare del Golfo beckoned.

We arrived bang on schedule to another effusive welcome. We were, after all, the second ever guests at Residence Aziyz.

Christmas in Sicily

We returned to Sciacca that Christmas for another week at Verdetecnica but this time we decided not to break the journey at Castellammare del Golfo. In an email Salvatore had warned us that the soon-to-be-inspected stilts on the main road north of Menfi remained soon-to-be-inspected so, having lunched at Marsala, we took our cross-country short cut and arrived in mid-afternoon; it was 22 December.

We exchanged some of our home-made Sardinian elixir for some of Pascale and Salvatore's home-made *limoncello* and then spent much of the next few days sitting in their house drinking both.

Christmas here was as we had hoped – understated. The shops were busy but almost the only concession to the season was a *poinsettia* on the threshold or just inside the door. In total we counted four Christmas trees and one of those was in Pascale and Salvatore's half-French home.

The first night, and almost every night thereafter, we ate at Santa Lucia. Francesca and family welcomed us in traditional Italian style and, as before, the boys helped her wait our table, a different table now, right next to a roaring fire. We asked about their opening plans over the Christmas period and, not as expected, Christmas Eve was the only problem;

Christmas at Verdetecnica

whereas on Christmas Day we could have *il pranzo* (lunch), but not *la cena* (dinner).

Every other restaurant seemed to be closed on Christmas Eve so we bought a ready-cooked chicken and a few vegetables at the market in Sciacca. When I said 'bought', as far as the vegetables were concerned that wasn't strictly true. I needed an onion and a pepper and decided to get them at different stalls. On both occasions when the stall holder realised I only wanted the one, he gave it to me and refused any money.

Christmas lunch at Santa Lucia was a curious affair, not because of the food but because of the company. There were two tables laid, one for Kay and me, the other for a party of eighteen. And that was it.

Our fellow guests turned out to be at least three generations of a large family: grandparents, their middle-aged children with their husbands and wives and all their grandchildren. Everyone was dressed very smartly and it was clear that *il nonno* (the grandfather) was in charge. He wasn't the first to enter the dining room but when he did, he immediately acknowledged our presence (as did his wife, *la nonna*) and wished us *Buon Natale*. Thereafter every other guest greeted us in the same fashion.

Since we first came to Italy we had eaten with or close to many family gatherings but this felt different. We weren't sure if it was a class thing, a status thing, a money thing, a suspicious thing or any other 'thing'; they were simply different, *particolare*. At first we thought it curious too that they were eating here on this particular day but then, basic local fare it might have been, but it was cooked with skill and passion and it showed. Perhaps somewhere along the line this family was a part of Francesca and Carlo's extended family.

We had all just finished our *antipasti* when one of the women, tall, elegant, sophisticated and dressed in black, stood up, left the table and purposefully walked across to our table.

'Do you speak English?' she said with an obvious American accent.

When we confessed that we did, she seemed relieved and then explained.

'I'm from Detroit', she said, 'my husband over there ... we met in Detroit when he first came to the US but now he's decided to return to Sicily to live. So here we are, my first Christmas in Sicily.'

And that was it. We had just time to tell her that we were on holiday, we'd been here before and were staying down the road before she said goodbye and returned to her table and her new family. Every so often she would catch our eye and give a smile of recognition or an almost clandestine wave of the fingers. A brief but intriguing encounter.

The meals progressed, we had all just finished our *primo piatto* when one of the younger sons (or older grandsons, it was difficult to tell) took out a packet of cigarettes and was just about to light up when *il nonno* admonished him and nodded in our direction, clearly indicating that we might not approve.

As he stood up to leave the dining room to have his cigarette outside, the offending male apologised to *il nonno* and also to us as he passed our table. Thereafter the smokers in the group excused themselves and headed out into the crisp Christmas sun.

No sooner had they all eaten, than they left. One-by-one they filed out and, as they passed our table, they all said goodbye to us in Italian, including the enigmatic wife from Detroit.

We stayed on a little longer and had a chat with Francesca and Carlo who went on to share some breaking news with us. They asked us if we knew the other, larger restaurant, La Traviata, on the road between Santa Lucia and Verdetecnica. We confessed that we had eaten there on our first visit, the first Tuesday when their place was shut; we were quick to add that we didn't enjoy the food and that we were the only people there that evening. All of which happened to be true.

Well, Francesca and Carlo had acquired La Traviata and early in the new year they would transfer the food and the ambience of Santa Lucia five hundred metres down the road. The four of us shared a celebratory drink.

As ever we revisited some of the places that we already knew and liked. Top of that list was Marsala where we stocked up with the local wine before heading along the coast road, the so-called Salt Road, in the direction of Trápani, to the Ettore e Infersa salt flats.

The technology of salt extraction was known to the ancient Egyptians but here it was the Greeks and Romans who developed the industry which reached its peak in the 19th century when salt from here flavoured or preserved food as far away as Norway and Russia; the windmills that supplied the energy to drain the water from the basins and to grind the salt were a mediæval development.

Today, with the industry in decline, the emphasis here has changed to facilitate those passing through, people like us, the tourists. The 16th century star-shaped Dutch windmill has been restored and there is a small museum, though the main Museo del Sale is housed in a three hundred year-old salt-worker's house further up the coast at Nubia.

This was the wrong time of year to see any serious activity – it is the hot summer sun that dries out the salt – but it was an exhilarating and enlightening diversion which caused us once again to miss out on whatever Trápani had to offer. Perhaps next time.

But we also ventured further afield and got as far as two of Sicily's most dramatic hill-top towns, Erice to the west and Enna to the east ... though not on the same day. The winding approach to both is striking and even intimidating, such commanding positions must have turned round many would-be predators. But we persevered and, at Enna, were rewarded with spectacular vistas, particularly across the valley to the neighbouring hill-top settlement of Calascibetta.

At Erice, it was the other way round we were struggling to see the top of the town as it was shrouded in a clinging, dank mist. We parked just inside the walls and climbed the narrow, well-paved mediæval streets. It was an eerie feeling, anywhere else and it might have had a sinister edge but here the small squares and decorated doorways were welcoming even in the gloom. Sometime we will have to return and see what Erice is really like.

There was one other hill-top town we visited, in certain lights visible from Verdetecnica. This was Caltabellotta, nine hundred metres up in the hills north and east of Sciacca, tucked in the shadow of a gigantic rock spur.

It rarely snows in this part of Sicily but that December was the exception and the road up to Caltabellotta offered even more spectacular views than usual. We had passed this way before in the summer and nicknamed it 'the grey town'. Now, with its greyness edged with a sharp white and illuminated by the precise winter sun, it was a spectacular view in itself but from the top there were amazing panoramas in every direction.

And I suppose that's why we visit these lofty towns, many of which, when you get there are basically the same – a castle, a cathedral, a few churches, small squares, big squares, blind alleyways, stepped alleyways, bars, a few shops. It's for the view. Not just the view from the top but the many vistas that are part of the climb. And when you get there, the reward is not just looking down on the lesser hills and plains or the distant sea – it's recognising where you've been, it's marvelling at the stilted road that brought you here, it's catching a glimpse of where you're staying, it's wondering what's in that field or beside that house, it's pointing to where you're going next, it's knowing that, soon, you'll be that speck down there.

It was our last night in Santa Lucia and we were eating at our usual table by the fire. It was a busy evening. A middle-aged Italian couple came in; we recognised them, like us they'd eaten here before. We nodded in recognition as Francesca showed them to the table next to ours. Francesca returned with the menus and there followed what can only be described as a heated discussion in fast, furious and animated Italian. And it was to do with us.

We didn't understand all of what was being said, but we got the gist of it – basically the woman was complaining that we always had the table by the fire. As politely and firmly as possible, Francesca explained that this was because we always got there first, at eight o'clock on the dot.

We were fairly certain that the displaced woman also brought our non-Italian-ness into the debate and that she asked Francesca what time we would be leaving, presumably so that they could swap tables. Her husband knew his place and refused to become involved ... all he wanted was to get on and eat.

I suppose it's possible that we got it all wrong, and it was just that they supported rival football teams or were discussing Berlusconi's latest clamp-down on the freedom of the press. But I doubt it. From time to time Francesca gave us some knowing looks and, of course, she could never be quite sure how much of the conversation we actually understood. Of one thing we were fairly certain – Francesca knew that this was our last night in Sciacca but she omitted to mention it to them.

As a gesture of solidarity, I turned round my chair to warm my hands at the fire for the last time. Next time we came to Sciacca we would be eating down the road at La Traviata*.

---

*Some months later I came across the following, an internet blog by an American woman who stayed at Verditecnica the following April:

'That night we headed up the mountain to a restaurant that had just opened that day, La Traviata. That day was their grand opening, and they did not have a lot of what was listed on the menu as the deliveries were to come the next day. With the waitress's small knowledge of English combined with our small knowledge of Italian we were able to put a meal together. We ordered Pasta alla Emiliana, which to my happy surprise was berette (flat spaghetti), peas and ham in a pink sauce. I thought pink sauce may be an American thing, I was pleasantly surprised to have found it in Sicily. It was delicious. I then had swordfish and my boyfriend had the shrimp speciality of the house. Everything was really good.'

We knew it was Francesca and Carlo's intention to re-open La Traviata on 15 January so something must have gone wrong ... thank goodness we had to cancel our original plan to return to Sciacca for a few days just to be at the opening!

Non c'è problema

It was after this visit to Sciacca that we decided to do something more about coming to grips with the language, *la lingua italiana*. Since our first visit to Italy we had been moderately successful at absorbing the basics, the day-to-day, meeting, greeting and eating stuff. But we felt that we relied too much on the universality of English and the fact that most Italians seemed to be able to fill in the gaps in *our* language when we got flummoxed in theirs. In short, we had evolved from knowing none to knowing some but not knowing enough.

Still, at least we were aware of our own shortcomings. Initially all we had was our wits, an ability to decipher the non-verbal language (which all Italians speak fluently), a couple of dictionaries, a well-worn BBC phrasebook and a sense of humour. But we knew this was not enough and regularly felt embarrassed at our lack of progress and the thought that, in this area, others might see us as stereotypical Brits abroad.

We spoke in infinitives, non-gender-specific adjectives and nouns – always in the singular – and a sprinkling of well-worn phrases, though sometimes in the wrong context.

To indicate that we wanted to eat, we would say *mangiare*

which actually means 'to eat'; for the word 'car', we would say *macchina* or maybe *macchino* without indicating the gender (it's feminine); we might tell someone we'd bought some apples but use the singular *mela* and not the plural *mele*; we would know that *stanco* meant tired but forget that Kay would be *stanca*; we knew that *è lontano?* meant 'is it far/long?' in terms of distance but sometimes we would use it when referring to time as in 'will it take long?' It's a wonder we ever found our way out of the airport.

The first faltering steps to do something about it came about when I heard someone on the radio mention the book-less language CDs of Michel Thomas. I bought the two-CD introductory course the following day and, as we wouldn't be returning to Italy for a few months, watched it gather dust until about a week before we set off.

But it did help, largely because it put some of what we already knew in context and, more importantly, introduced us to the present tense, real verbs that put the infinitives (like *mangiare*, to eat) behind us and changed our lives with:

mangio (I eat / I am eating)

mangia (she, he or it eats /is eating) and

mangiamo (we eat / are eating)

Mangiano (they eat / are eating) didn't figure initially. And that, in turn, gave us a future tense as, more often than not, the present tense doubles as the future in Italian – *mangio oggi* means 'I am eating today' and *mangio stasera* means 'I *will* eat this evening'. (There is actually a future tense as well which is used for more specific events in the future.)

Of course, when we next went to Italy armed with our new-found tense, we just had to use it at every opportunity ... yes, it was only the present tense but at least it was a step up from the lowly infinitive! And, give them their due, Italians coped well with our new version of their language and quickly adapted to the notion that, in our world, the present tense could be used for past, present and future, a world where *mangiamo* could mean we ate, we have eaten, we eat, we will eat or anything else to do with us eating yesterday, today or tomorrow. It was a simplistic linguistic breakthrough that might not have made total sense but in most cases *could* be understood and, as far as we know, never led to any unfortunate diplomatic incidents.

It would be great to report that, as we progressed through the CDs (we later acquired all eight of the basic course), we became almost fluent. Sadly it wasn't like that, mainly because we lead busy lives when we're not in Italy and we're only actually there a total of four to five weeks a year.

That said, we could (and still can) see areas where we have improved though, paradoxically, this has also made us more aware of our shortcomings. Every time we went to Italy we would have the same conversation about how little progress we had made ... but, by the time we left, we knew we were a little better. Ironically, we often found ourselves apparently struggling more towards the end of the holiday but I think that's because we were more confident and were trying to get our heads round more complicated ideas like the past tense or trying to work out how reflexive verbs work.

Above all else we realised it's the verbs, the cement of any language, that are the key – once you've got the patterns of the regular verbs and understand how *avere* (to have) and *essere* (to be) work, then you're halfway there and have earned the right to make mistakes with the irregular verbs. Indeed it's a sign of progress and a degree of understanding if you say the Italian equivalent of 'teached' rather than 'taught'.

For me the process of picking up the language, has been peppered with key moments, though I did not necessarily recognise them as such at the time; similarly there were things

127

I wished I had assimilated earlier in the process, things that would have made life much easier.

Here, then, is a totally non-linguistic and personal guide to picking up the language and one pronunciation Eureka moment that changed everything. It goes without saying that we still can't speak Italian but we do speak it badly, better.

Start counting. This is top of the list because we failed to do it early on and even now still have problems. On one occasion, aboard a plane to Italy, we sat next to a teacher of Italian (an Italian herself) and she told us that counting was the one thing she insisted that all her pupils could do parrot-fashion. She's right ... I could do it in German and French almost without thinking, yet continued to struggle with Italian. Here's some of the reasons it's so important:

You can have a phone conversation. Think of how often numbers come up when you're on the phone; I'm quite happy to make a phonecall in Germany but know I would shy away from it in Italy ... and I know why.

You can shop – you can barter at markets, you can say how much you want and can understand the cost of your supermarket shopping without waiting for the electronic price to appear at the check-out, you can pay the right money and get the right change.

You can follow directions which often include numbers ... and then you can give directions.

You can tell and understand the time, the date, the year.

You can tell people how old you are, when your birthday is, how many children you have and how old they are.

You can tell the difference between *diciotto* (eighteen) and *ottanta* (eighty).

Dabble in a course. Language learning courses such as the Michel Thomas one can be bought at most bookshops ... but

by far the cheapest way to get hold of one
don't get on with it you can re-sell it on eBa
if you do get on with it you can copy it and
I'd call that a win-win situation!

Find a phrase. The first phrase we learnt (and could pronounce) was *non c'è problema* (the *c'è* is pronounced *tchay* and means 'there is') which means 'no problem' and we used it even when there was a problem. It's a wonderfully simple phrase with so many applications and it made us feel good. It was *our* phrase! We even used it in England.

Other useful ones for us were: *come si dice ...?*, how do you say ...?; *quattro anni / mesi / settimane / giorni / ore fa*, four years / months / weeks / days / hours *ago* (or any other number); *secondo me ...*, in my opinion ...; *il pieno per favore*, fill it up please; and the aforementioned *è lontano?*, is it far?

And then there's my favourite one-word phrase, one word that encapsulates many and varied ideas in Italian. It's *posso?* with questioning intonation, a questioning look and, more often than not, a pointing finger. In a restaurant it might mean 'Can I sit here' or 'Is this table free?'. In a shop it could mean, 'Can I have a closer look at this?' or 'Can I try this on?' Basically it's the same as 'Can / may I?' in English but is used much more often in Italian.

There is something very satisfying about being able to string a couple of words together and it gives you confidence for the next big step ... a whole sentence!

Become weather-wise. When we learnt the words to do with the weather we found we could have whole conversations with complete strangers. When we started to throw in *oggi* (today) or *domani* (tomorrow) or even *dopodomani* (the day after tomorrow), we could almost have got a job on Italian television.

ıe simple weather words are: *caldo* (warm/hot), *freddo* old), *fresco* (cool/fresh), *il sole* (sun), *la pioggia* (rain), *la nebbia* (fog), *il vento* (wind), *la nuvola* (cloud). Add *troppo* (too / too much) or *molto* (very, a lot) and there's a verbless sentence in the making.

Scorcio has nothing to do with the weather, it means the end or close of a season or a period of time.

Eavesdrop. Not surprisingly we always understood a lot more that we could ever communicate in speech. That time in Santa Lucia when the woman was ranting and raving about us sitting by the fire, we understood what was going on but, if she had turned and spoken to us, we would have been dumbfounded and struck dumb at the same time ... and probably just said, *non c'è problema*.

We're both particularly good eavesdroppers and the Italians make it easy by using their hands so much when they talk. I don't think I've ever heard an Italian whisper ... perhaps because they would have to move their hands ever so slowly.

Pick up the patterns. All Italian words end in a vowel, so if it doesn't it's wrong or perhaps, just perhaps, it's actually a foreign word that has crept into Italian (for example, *un film western* or *trendy*), in which case, you'll know it anyway. Some older Italians can't handle such modern 'foreign' words that don't end in a vowel, so they stick one on the end just to be on the safe side.

Most English nouns that end in '-tion' are almost the same in Italian but the 't' becomes a 'z' and there's an 'e' on the end – *la posizione*, *la situazione*, *la reputazione* – notice the gender.

Most English adjectives that end in '-ant' and '-ent' are the same in Italian but with an 'e' on the end – *importante*, *ignorante*, *pertinente*, *apparente*.

There are many such patterns that relate directly to English words and their endings and when you spot one of them (like words ending in '-ical'), you'll find lots of examples. But, as you might expect, there are a few false friends and, if you decide that *una camera* means a camera, *actuale* means actual or that *sensibile* means sensible*, so what? They're not hanging offences** and might just bring a smile to somebody's face when you get it wrong.

Learn how to say Sciacca. Some Italian words, like Sciacca or *cerchio* (circle), just look so strange and unpronounceable. Over the years I've given this a lot of thought and have concluded that it's the letter 'c' that is the problem. Crack the letter 'c' and you've almost cracked Italian pronunciation.

There was a time when I would look at a word with 'c's and work out which of the four possibilities it was and then make a stab at it:

- as in English, if the 'c' is followed by 'a', 'o' or 'u', it is pronounced hard as in 'cat';
- before 'e' or 'i' it has a softer 'tch' sound (in fact the 't' is hardly pronounced at all);
- 'ch' is like the 'k' in 'kit';
- 'sc' before 'e' or 'i' is pronounced 'sh'.

So *cerchio* is *(t)ch-er-kio*; and Sciacca is *shia-ca*.

It's a few years now since I cracked the Italian c-words and, in so doing, freed up the ever-expanding how-to-pronounce-Italian space in my brain. For the first time I felt confident that I could pronounce the names of all the signposted towns and villages that we drove past ... and to prove the point

---

*For the record, *una camera* means a room (a camera is *una macchina fotografica)*; *actuale* means present (actual is *effettivo)*; *sensibile* means sensitive (sensible is *ragionevole)*.

**There is one near-hanging-offence clanger that you *can* make in Italian which involves the word for fig (*il fico*); it's really important to get the gender right here – see page 155 for a more explicit explanation.

would do so out loud and with unrestrained relish at every opportunity ... Roccella, Bianchi, Cicala, Scigliano ...

Read the signs. Following on from the basics of being able to read (and pronounce) road signs is the whole sign culture which is an endemic part of Italian life. There are signs everywhere and, apart from passing on important information, they are a rich source of handy phrases and new vocabulary that can be transferred to other situations: *centro storico* (historical centre), *senso unico* (one-way), *senso vietato* or *vietato l'ingresso* (no entry), *lavori in corso* (roadworks), *strada senza uscita* (cul-de-sac/no exit), *l'ufficio postale* (post office), *curva pericolosa* (dangerous bend), *vietato fumare* (no smoking), *campo di calcio* (football stadium), *spiaggia privato* (private beach).

Invest in a good dictionary. At the time of writing we have bought at least four English-Italian/Italian-English dictionaries ... and we will shortly invest in a fifth. The first was a useful pocket-sized mini dictionary, as was the second as I forgot to pack the first one and had to buy another when we got to Italy. We graduated to a middle-sized dictionary with some useful pages about grammar and verbs; this was a good buy.

The largest tome, the Cassell's dictionary, was bought second-hand and was a waste of the little money it cost. I was blinded by its size and eventually by the small print ... what I didn't pick up at the time was that it was about thirty years old and, as such, completely out of date (*scaduto*); out of date with reference to technology is *superato* and does not even get a mention in this 1128-page dictionary.

On re-reading these pages I realise I may have given the impression that we speak Italian reasonably well now. Nothing could be further from the truth. Our vocabulary has clearly expanded and we *know* a lot more about the language but when we get down to the nitty-gritty we just muddle through. We take a few steps forward, then one back and never did what we always said we would – practise in between visits to Italy, well not until the last minute, that is.

Yes, on occasions some Italians lied and said that we speak their language well but we know they're either just being incredibly polite or have forgotten to plug in their hearing aid. Still, even when you know it's not true, at least someone has acknowledged that you made an effort.

That said, we never tire of listening to Italian being spoken and would dearly love to have more control over our attempts at conversation. Perhaps one day we will and it'll all fall into place; in the meantime, *non c'è problema!*

Bari

Adriatic Sea

Alberobello

Ostuni

Brindisi

APULIA

Taranto

Lecce

Leverano

Porto Cesareo

Galatina

CORIGLIANO
D'OTRANTO

SOGLIANO

Maglie

Otranto

Gulf of Taranto

Gallipoli

Cutrofiano

Brindisi to Bari · 110km

134

Heading into the heel

We don't usually watch any of the television travel programmes but flicking through the channels early one evening we came across some celebrity or other taking a paid-for break in Apulia.

Not surprisingly the programme focused on Alberobello, the town, with its quaint circular *trulli*, that could easily have been a body double for Hobbitsville in *Lord of the Rings*. Unconvinced by *trulli-turismo*, it nevertheless did serve to remind us that here was a part of southern Italy that we'd never even considered as a holiday destination. The Ryanair website beckoned. Flights to Bríndisi had just started from Stansted so we started to search for somewhere to stay in the heel of Italy, the part of Apulia known as the Salento.

We were looking for somewhere right in the centre of the heel, with the sea more or less equidistant on three sides and found a *villetta* near the small town of Sogliano Cavour, between Galatina and Maglie. Paula, the owner, relied on her friend Francesca to communicate with us in English so all the final arrangements were made through her. We would catch the evening flight to Bríndisi, stay overnight in a hotel and drive down to Galatina the next day where we'd meet up with Francesca and Paula around three in the afternoon.

For the first time we were going to spend a little over a fortnight in Italy. It was June.

We had booked in to Bríndisi's Hotel Torino and were clutching the directions as we turned off the *autostrada* and on to the Via Appia and headed into town. The directions were all based on turning left or right at *il semaforo* (traffic lights) and the first three went according to plan ... the final direction was, 'turn left at the fourth set of lights and take the first right and you'll see the Hotel Torino in front of you'.

So far so good ... one set ... two sets ... three sets ... it's bound to be the next ones ... but the next ones never came. Almost before we realised it, we were driving down a wide two-lane thoroughfare lined with shops and bars which had clearly been pedestrianised for the evening. And we were behind a police car *and* in the left-hand lane.

The people of Bríndisi were out walking in the balmy evening air, the *passeggiata** was in full summer swing; apart from giving it a wide berth, nobody seemed to give the police car and its attendant hire car a second glance ... perhaps they thought we were on 'plain clothes' duty. Perhaps even the *polizia* in front of us thought we were on 'plain clothes' duty.

Our private little convoy continued towards the sea which we could now see a hundred metres or so ahead. As we approached the end of the *corso* the police car slowed; we followed suit.

It stopped. We stopped about ten metres behind.

The passenger side of the police car opened. A uniformed policeman stepped out, donned his cap and purposefully

---

*The *passeggiata* is an Italian tradition. It is a leisurely pre-prandial early evening walk when friends and relatives stroll and chat and, sometimes, do a little business; a chance to see and be seen. The *passeggiata* is as much a feature of a large city as it is of a small town or village. See pages 221 and 253 for more detailed encounters with the *passeggiata*.

adjusted the crutch of his trousers, a sure sign that he meant business.

I suggested to Kay that we go into 'dumb tourist' mode and prepare to apologise profusely for being on the wrong side of this closed-off road. As the policeman was on her side of the car, I was expecting (hoping?) that she'd have to do the talking.

The policeman glanced in our direction and then strode off to his right and embraced a friend in the middle of the road. They talked, they laughed, they waved their arms, they shrugged, they shook hands. They ignored us.

Greetings and chit-chat over, the policeman returned to his car and it drove off. Naturally we followed. We both turned left along the seafront. They carried on, we turned left again, parked up and wondered where the hell we were and what had happened to that fourth set of traffic lights.

So it was time to switch on the satellite navigation ... otherwise known as my sense of direction. I knew roughly where we should have been so started to head back 'inland' and, as far as possible, parallel to Bríndisi's main thoroughfare. We stopped once to ask directions and were given accurate and precise instructions which included going up a one-way street the wrong way. Who were we to argue? ... we did as instructed and it did the trick. Five minutes later we pulled up outside Hotel Torino.

When we'd signed in, I asked about the traffic lights; the man on reception shrugged his shoulders in fluent Italian and explained that the lights had been removed some three weeks earlier. Unfortunately the directions on the website had not yet been updated. Several years on, this remains the case ... unless, of course, the fourth set has now been replaced!

We had a few hours to kill in Bríndisi before we set off for our rendezvous in Galatina. A chance to window-shop and work out how it was that we'd ended up driving down the pedestrianised Corso Garibaldi the night before.

But I had another mission. I was desperate to get my hair cut but I was being choosy; I lingered outside and scrutinised several places looking for *un barbiere* I would entrust with this special task. Truth be known, I was looking for somewhere with no-one in the chair and no waiting customers so that I would be less embarrassed as I tried to explain what I wanted. My search ended in the Piazza Cairoli; I took a deep breath and entered, left to my fate by Kay who had noticed a few interesting shops close by.

This barber's nickname was *il lampo*, the speedy one, though it was Kay who found that out when she got into conversation with a local shopkeeper and explained where I was. I, on the other hand, was experiencing it at first hand.

After we'd got beyond that and-what-would-sir-like-today moment and I'd done my best to explain my simple needs, *il lampo* positioned himself behind by left ear and shot round to the other side through a blur of hands, comb, scissors and hair – the latter shot up into the air before descending to the floor. He could probably tell from my gobsmacked reflection in the mirror that I'd never experienced anything like this before, so he did it again, and again, at different levels. I kept very still ... it crossed my mind that one slip and he'd have a bit of an ear off.

It was undoubtedly the most unusual and spectacular haircut I had ever had and, what's more, the end result was exactly what I wanted. When he had finished and I was coughing up my €9 he answered my puzzled expression by pointing to a certificate on the wall and explaining that he had trained in Milan to acquire this special technique.

Still in a state of shock, I stumbled back into the sun and into Kay and told her about my unique hairdressing experience; she was unimpressed, she already knew all about him. Still, I decided there and then that in two weeks time, when we would return to Bríndisi, I would have another haircut here and Kay could see for herself.

Just after lunch we headed south from Bríndisi, drove around the outskirts of Lecce and headed to Galatina where we had lunch. As arranged, just before three o'clock, we phoned Francesca. She and Paula soon arrived and we followed them to Sogliano.

Paula was dark and slim and looked far too young to have a property to rent out. Francesca was blonde and bubbly, she was a little older than Paula, spoke fluent English (we later found out that she'd lived in London for eight years) and was clearly enjoying her role as itinerant translator.

Paula's *villetta* was not in Sogliano itself but in open countryside just off the road midway between Cutrofiano and Corigliano d'Otranto and when we arrived we were greeted by the rest of her family, her mother and father and two brothers. It was clear we were a bit of a novelty; we were their first English-speaking guests and we were also staying for a fortnight which was unusual enough to explain the 'red carpet' treatment. We guessed too that there may not have been any guests here since the previous summer – most Italians tend to holiday in August.

The house was a single-storey building standing in its own small plot bordered by a low unfinished wall. It was clean and tidy, albeit featureless, and could easily have slept six or more so we rattled around a bit. The least appealing area was the hotchpotch of a kitchen but, as we weren't ever going to cook, except for breakfast and some fruit and cheese for lunch, that wasn't a huge problem.

Francesca, pointed us in the direction of the two nearest *supermercati*, one in Corigliano d'Otranto and one near Cutrofiano, where she lived and worked in her brother's small jewellery shop; she also told us there was a restaurant on the road to Cutrofiano.

After we'd unpacked and checked that there was a corkscrew in the kitchen (there was, but there were no knives until we called Francesca), we headed for Corigliano d'Otranto to stock up with the essentials of life – red wine, coffee, milk, bottled water, bread, fruit and cheese. Laden we walked as far as the arch by the castle, then back to the car and back to base to enjoy the late afternoon sun. Following that first trip into Corigliano it was always at the back of our minds that some day we should return and explore what lay beyond the arch. Corigliano felt like an interesting little town and we did eventually go back, though we wished we had done so sooner.

That evening we returned to Galatina to eat – the restaurant that Francesca had told us about was closed and, anyway, we didn't really think that a large, modern, featureless monstrosity called Fanny's was the place for us. By contrast, in the back alleys of Galatina we discovered the Borgo Antico and ate there most nights thereafter – excellent, nay superb, *antipasti*, excellent *primi e secundi piatti*, another small family-run restaurant.

This was the end of our first day in the heart of the Salento which, as we expected, was quite different from any other part of Italy we'd been to – it was flat and, except for the area around Bríndisi, totally riverless. Around the coastal perimeter we expected to find a more undulating landscape but here, in the central plateau, it was as flat as a pancake, sometimes boringly so.

So, it's all the more surprising that this was the part of Italy we were to visit most frequently. The Salento was where we'd get to know a lot of people and where, when we were nostalgic for Italy, our thoughts would turn. It all began a week later when we finally stopped off in Corigliano d'Otranto and encountered Gino ...

But first we had a car to return to Bríndisi *Aeroporto* – we'd noticed something dripping from the working end so took it back and picked up another one. As we'd come this far it seemed impertinent not to explore north and west of Bríndisi and, against all our instincts, take a look at Hobbitsville, *trulli*-town Alberobello.

We headed initially for the more undulating terrain beyond the northern reaches of the Salento and the whitewashed hill-town of Ostuni. It was a blistering hot day and Ostuni, white and bright in the heat haze, dominated the landscape as we wound our slow way up through ancient terraced olive groves. Unusually for us we parked in one of the lower car parks and negotiated the Moorish maze of narrow *vicoli*, through arches, up stone steps and past whitewashed buildings that lead to the *centro storico*. When we stepped out into the *piazza*, we were almost poleaxed by a wall of heat; it was as if the whiteness was reflecting and compounding the unrelenting heat of the sun. It was the cusp of the *siesta*; shutters rattled down and keys were turned, cigarettes were lit and scooters sprang into life and headed out of town. We took the hint and slowly made for the shade of the nearest café to rehydrate, watch the world go by in black and white and gird our loins for what lay ahead.

This was the gateway to *trulli**-country and, in retrospect, we wished that we had stopped here at the gate and not headed north to Alberobello. But head north we did and en route we

---

*The origin and meaning of the name *trulli* is not known; what is known is that since the 14th century these circular whitewashed houses made with mortar-less blocks of limestone and topped with conical roofs have become a unique feature of the Apulian landscape north-west of Ostuni.

Trulli rooftops in Alberobello

passed several *trulli* in various states of repair; some looking run-down, some newly painted and lived in, sometimes just one in a field, sometimes clusters of two, three and more. These *trulli* were interesting and photogenic, quaint intrusions dotted here and there in a sparkling summery landscape.

At Alberobello, on the other hand, somebody was breeding them, around 1500 of them to be precise. I reckon that Peter Jackson missed a trick here when he made the *Lord of the Rings* trilogy – the set for the Hobbit village already existed here in Alberobello. That said, it might have cost him more for this town knew when it was on to a good thing and every nook and cranny of the town was geared to exploiting *trulli*-ism. In addition to the normal gift and craft shops and places to eat (all housed in *trulli*), there were places to stay and 'open' houses and balconies with panoramic views of even more *trulli*.

I'm ashamed to admit it, but we fell for one of the latter. Our would-be host was standing in the doorway to his little shop and, spotting our cameras, said that we could take some photos from his terrace, one of the best panoramas of Alberobello. We thought he was just being friendly in the way we had come to expect of Italians in non-*trulli* Italy. And, yes, the views were special ... how often in a lifetime do you see the rooftops of fifteen hundred *trulli*? But there was a price to pay ... getting out of the building without buying something. We were pursued round the little shop as we feigned interest in this and that and all the time trying to subtly edge our way towards the door. But our hand-wringing host was *trulli* nimble and always seemed to be able to position himself between us and our only means of escape.

In retrospect, what we should have done was make a bolt back up to the rooftop terrace (that would have surprised him) and leapt Bond-like from *trulli* roof to *trulli* roof before sliding down to terra-firma as if nothing had happened. Instead we gave in and re-emerged into the sun clutching a bottle of some over-priced drink and bemoaning our weakness.

People come to Alberobello in coachloads and carloads. We wondered just how many, like us, vacated the large car parks *trulli* disappointed?

Leaps of faith

Over the next ten days or so we saw a lot more of Francesca and also met up with her boyfriend, Ciccio. We spent a typical 'youthful' Italian evening with them when, after they both finished work (around nine in the evening, very late for us), we went to eat at a *mazzeria* (an old farm-cum-restaurant, many of which are part of the *agriturismo* network) and then drove on to the coast at Porto Cesareo for a balmy late night stroll and a *gelato*.

But memorable though this evening was, it was our lunchtime invitation to eat with Francesca, her brother, Salvatore, and her parents, Attilio and Silvana, that introduced us to a less predictable Italian sub-culture.

We met up with Francesca outside the shop in Cutrofiano and she drove us the couple of kilometres into the neighbouring countryside to the small single-storey farm that was home. Attilio, robust and weathered from years of hard outdoor work and wearing shorts and a vest that looked like permanent fixtures, and Silvana, a comfortable, florid, no-nonsense housewife who knew how to keep her man in his place, welcomed us like long-lost children.

Introductions over, Silvana swung into action in the

kitchen, while Attilio and Francesca showed us round the adjoining small plot of land that the family worked. Here they grew anything and everything that could be put on the table and also kept a few chickens and pigs in outhouses away from the house. Kay and Attilio were soon talking the same market gardening language aided and abetted by Francesca's translations. I was nodding and trying to remember all the Italian names for the vegetables.

The one local crop conspicuous by its absence here was *tobacco*. Galatina was an important centre of the Italian tobacco industry and, locally, we had come to recognise the plant's broad leaves. When I mentioned this to Attilio he shook his head, he didn't want to have anything to do with the tobacco industry; Francesca looked uncomfortable as she fiddled with her lighter.

Although this was a working environment, there were pockets of shade and corners of buildings where time had stood still; where an unused bucket, a length of pipe, a coil of wire or an antiquated tool lay abandoned, sometimes gathering foliage and a dusting of the rich red earth, perhaps awaiting a second chance. I spotted a makeshift canopy adjoining the side of the house and, curious, took a closer look; I thought as much … this was where Attilio kept his Apé.

I'd always fancied having a go in an Apé (Italian for 'bee') one of those three-wheeled utilitarian farm vehicles that buzz about all over the southern Italian countryside, often packed with people rather than produce, more often people *and* produce and always just in front of you on those winding mountainous roads. Surely 'How many people can you cram into an Apé?' must eventually become a challenge for the *Guinness Book of Records*.

Truth be told, I did toy with the idea of asking Attilio if I could take his Apé out for a spin until I noticed it was laden with vegetables that I assumed he would sell. Perhaps another time.

Salvatore still hadn't put in an appearance when Francesca summoned us to the table.

This was a working household; the kitchen and adjacent dining room were extensions of the garden and its produce. They were not showcases and had probably remained unchanged for decades, a place of old, dark, functional furniture and few airs and graces. As we sat ourselves round the table, Salvatore rushed in, made his apologies and fell into the waiting chair ... just as Francesca was subtly warning us that her father was about to say 'grace'.

Formalities out of the way, we tucked in to *orecchietti** in a tomato sauce followed by a rich meat stew accompanied by bread, vegetables, potatoes and red wine and rounded off with the regulation *torta* we had brought with us – the latter almost the only thing that was not home-grown or home-made.

Francesca was our interpreter as we extolled the virtues of this down-to-earth *cucina tipica* and made sure that both Attilio and Silvana knew how much we appreciated their hospitality, their kindness and their hard work. The eating over, Attilio went to the tall, glass-fronted sideboard and took out another bottle of red wine and offered it to us. We took this as a signal that we should be on our way ... we were aware that we were encroaching on their time of rest, *la siesta.* Clutching our bottle of Attilio's best red, Francesca drove us back to our car in Cutrofiano.

This short journey was full of surprises as Francesca

---

*Small ear-shaped pasta that are an Apulian speciality. Most areas have at least one pasta that it can call its own – *fregola,* for example, is really only found in Sardinia. Apulia has a second, *fenescecchie*, strips of pasta wound into tight spirals.

explained that her mother and father (and most of her family) were Jehovah's Witnesses, apparently the second largest religion in Italy*. Apart from the 'grace', this revelation seemed somehow out of step with our lunchtime experience so we interrogated Francesca accordingly. What about the wine and the drinking ... we thought that Jehovah's Witnesses didn't imbibe? Francesca explained that, as she understood it, they could drink but not get drunk – a plausible, if unlikely, rationale. We pressed on ... what about the door-to-door bit? (it was difficult to imagine Attilio in a suit) ... yes, they did that too and her father *did* wear a suit on such occasions.

It was all rather bizarre, mostly because it didn't fit in with our experience. I suppose the answer was that these were Italian Jehovah's Witnesses and our only encounters had been with the UK branch. The cultural and historic influences were different and so too was the end result ... Italian Jehovah's Witnesses who enjoyed their red wine and might even pinch your bottom if you'd convert!

Eight years of living and working in London had 'cleansed' Francesca of her parents' religious bent and, she confessed, there were often areas of conflict which could lead to periods of little or no communication. We liked Francesca a lot and shared some of the anguish and frustration she experienced through a simple need to be allowed to think for herself. Attilio and Silvana had made us very welcome, over and above the call of duty ... we wondered later how they would

---

*I found this assertion difficult to get my head round and checked it out on the internet when we returned to England. It was correct; in 2003 it was estimated that there were 400,000 Jehovah's Witnesses in Italy and therefore, in numerical terms, it was the second religion to Roman Catholicism. Other research in this area suggested that, of all religions, Roman Catholicism was the most likely to supply a fertile pool of recruits to the Jehovah's Witnesses; one document argues that this is because 'both religions continue to blindly follow the organisation in spite of major doctrinal changes, reversals and flip-flops' and that 'both view every other church as heretical and false'.

have coped had they known that they had had two heathens in their midst helping them not get drunk. I would like to think that, as friends of Francesca, they would have treated us no differently.

Paola and her family were also Jehovah's Witnesses and it was through the local JW network that Paola knew that Francesca could speak English and, decadent or not, her language skills would prove useful in the holidays-for-heathens business.

But there was one other revelation to come. The meat Silvana had so lovingly prepared for us was *cavallo*, horse … though, of course, we didn't know it at the time. Back in Cutrofiano, we leapt out of the car, whinnied and waved *ciao* to Francesca.

We had already noticed that *cavallo* was a feature of most Apulian menus – we later ate in one place where, apart from *salsicce* (sausages) it was the *only* meat on the menu; naturally we had the sausages. It was some months later that the penny dropped … it had never occurred to us at the time that the *salsicce* might just be left-over-pieces-of-horse sausages!

To a meat-eater, what is the difference between eating horse as opposed to, say, cow, pig or sheep? It must be simply cultural. In the UK horses are on the 'domestic' side of the continuum along with cats and dogs *and* they generally have names; in parts of southern of Italy and in some other European countries they straddle the borderline between domestic and livestock. To expect Italians in such areas not to eat horse meat is like suggesting he or she should give up onions or olives; it is, they would argue, lean, protein-rich, finely textured, bright red and firm … and completely BSE-free.

And, I can testify, it is very tasty … though I don't think I could eat a whole one.

We asked Francesca about *zanzare* (mosquitos) and the best way to keep the little buggers from biting. I'd never really been troubled with them before but in Paola's house they were an unwelcome guest and for some reason I was their favourite host.

I showed Francesca my hands. On the back of the left one we counted fourteen bites ... and then there was the other hand and my arms and legs, it was impossible to even estimate how many times I had been bitten; thankfully my face must have frightened them away.

We bought a couple of plug-in repellents and Paola (to whom Francesca must have spoken) turned up with even more and enough of the little blue replacement pads to see us through to the end of the holiday. Whether it was these that did the trick or the fact that there was little room left on my body to bite, we'll never know but *zanzare* soon became less of a problem. Next time we'd come prepared.

We continued to eat in Galatina until we hit a snag, the Borgo Antico was going to be closed for a few days. We made a fruitless sortie into Cutrofiano in search of somewhere to eat but drew a blank so off we went again to the much larger Galatina.

It was the evening of the Italy–Sweden game in the Euro 2004 football Championships and the main *piazza* boasted a large screen and tiered seating for the occasion. At first we were only interested in finding somewhere to eat and so approached the local policeman, *il vigile*, who initially shook his head before having second thoughts. He asked us to wait where we were and strode off purposefully through the gathering crowds and down a side street. On his return he motioned to us to follow him and led us to La Tarantella, a modern eatery with its decor and ambience totally devoted to the rituals associated with the frenzied dance that supposedly followed the bite of a spider, the Salentine phenomenon of *tarantismo**.

Back in the square we eavesdropped on the rest of the football from the sidelines and wondered why so many people chose to watch the game here. Almost all would have had access to a television and yet they chose to come out into the town and watch their national team play in this communal atmosphere. When it was all over, the good-natured supporters dispersed into the cafés and bars; most seemed happy enough with the 1–1 draw. Four days later it was a different story.

---

*The origins of this half religious, half mythological superstition are in the bite of the Salentine *tarantula* which, unlike others, was supposedly venomous. The women 'bitten' (it was mainly women), the *tarantati*, would display hallucinogenic symptoms and feel the need to sweat the poison from their system by embarking upon a non-stop frenzied dance to the haunting and incessant accompaniment of violin and tambourine. Sometimes the 'dancing' went on for days until the *tarantati* fell to the ground exhausted but liberated from the supposed spells caused by the spider's bite. In reality the offending spider, if indeed there was one, was more likely to have been the black widow.

Other respected sources suggest that many depressed, frustrated and subordinate women became *tarantati* to 'cure' themselves by becoming, for a time, the centre of attention.

Not surprisingly the church embraced the ritual and made it its own. In Galatina it is still remembered every June during the feast of St Peter and St Paul, those well-known cleansers of all things venomous.

A balcony in Corigliano d'Otranto

Corigliano d'Otranto and beyond

At long last we ventured beyond Corigliano d'Otranto's stone arch by the castle and discovered a town that we couldn't quite figure out or quantify.

There were the usual understated shops and unpretentious bars scattered along narrow, well-kept streets radiating from a small square complete with fountain. With Borgo Antico still closed, we were keeping an eye out for somewhere to eat later in the evening and saw a few signs on walls but not much activity. We stood outside the castle and read the information board that explained about the nine 'Greek' towns, La Grecia Salentina, dotted around a small area between Lecce and Maglie. Corigliano d'Otranto was one of the nine.

We walked back towards the arch and had just sat down outside the Bar del Arco for a drink when Kay spotted a small card in the window offering short-term accommodation to rent. We asked the waitress for some more information but she didn't know any more than was on the card so she made a call. Five minutes later a car drew up and out skipped a short, sprightly, bright-eyed and moustached Italian, cigarette in one hand, mobile in the other; he skipped over to our table (didn't take him long to spot the foreigners) and introduced himself as Gino, the owner of the bar.

Gino asked us if we were looking for accommodation in the town or in the countryside. We explained it was the latter we were more interested in but not for now ... it was for some time in the future, maybe later in the year, maybe next year. Two minutes later and we were heading out of town in Gino's car, out on the road to Galatina where we turned down a narrow lane, then onto a track.

Gino's piece of land, in an area called Colombe, housed two purpose-built semi-detached bungalows. One was occupied, so he showed us round the other and explained that they were the same, *uguali*.

In our heads we were comparing and contrasting with our accommodation down the road in Sogliano. This was smaller inside but larger outside. As well as possible neighbours, the environs included a substantial plot where Gino cultivated vegetables and an outhouse with chickens; there were areas of shade, places to sit and places to lie, a verandah, flowers, little unkempt stone walls, a grassed area, a hammock slung up between a couple of trees. Inside, it was small but both the bathroom and kitchen were modern, clean and practical. There was no doubt about it, this is where we would have preferred to have been staying.

Gino was in his element. He knew he'd created a quirky little enclave in the Salentine countryside and he could see we liked it here. Just before we returned to Corigliano he reached up into a tree, picked three *fichi* (figs) and gave us one each. As he ate his and Kay tucked into hers he was extolling their ripeness and their wondrous taste while I was trying to change the subject back to the chickens he had just shown us.

I hated figs – mine was still in my hand like an unexploded hand grenade; I pulled the pin and surreptitiously ditched it before 'accidentally' stepping on it. Unfortunately Gino witnessed my irrational act and, taken in by my obvious disappointment, plucked an even larger and riper one from the tree. *'Non c'è problema'*, he quipped as he stuffed it into my ungrateful hand.

I'd disliked figs since the first time I bit into a dry, gritty, tasteless fig roll as a child. If blandness were in need of a simile, then 'fig roll' would do the trick: as bland as a fig-roll, as tasteless as a fig roll, as pointless as a fig roll ... they all work for me. I'd given them a go once or twice since but still couldn't get on with them ... fig rolls, that is. I'd never actually tasted a fig in the flesh, so to speak.

We were driving back to the bar. I was sitting in the front beside Gino and he noticed that I still hadn't tucked into my fig. In faltering Italian I tried to say that I was saving it for later, *puì tarde* (when I might be nearer a rubbish bin or a field) but he countered by telling me that it wouldn't stay at its best for long. I had run out of excuses and knew I would have to do it. I was already wincing with anticipation as I peeled and bit into my first fig ... and in seconds my wince had become a grin and then a smile. Gino was right, this was a to-die-for taste and texture that I'd never experienced and had always steadfastly avoided; I realised then what I'd been missing all those years.

I'd also learnt a new Italian word, *fico*, a masculine word that could get the unsuspecting and non-gender-aware foreigner into all sorts of linguistic trouble. There is another, similar, word, a feminine word with an 'a' at the end that has a completely different meaning, the equivalent to what English speakers would call the 'c-word'.

For what it's worth, my advice is to buy pre-packed figs in a *supermercato* or, if you have to have fresh at a market stall, keep your mouth shut and just point in Italian!

Of course I hate fig rolls even more now!

Back at Bar del Arco we asked Gino how much it would be to rent one of his little bungalows and he shrugged his shoulders as if that were a mere technicality but, when pressed, plucked forty-euros-a-day out of the ether. He knew we'd flown to Bríndisi and added that, if we did indeed return to stay in Corigliano, he'd pick us up at the airport and find us a car when we got here.

Before we left Corigliano that afternoon we quizzed Gino about somewhere to eat and he directed us to at least half a dozen places, none of which we had spotted on our walk round the town.

Early evening and we were back in Corigliano and, sure enough, little restaurants had popped up all over the place. The roads around the square were closed to traffic and tables, chairs, potted shrubs, trellis, candles and lights had spilled out onto even the narrowest of streets. We were spoilt for choice and were confident we'd soon find the one for us, 'our' restaurant in Corigliano.

For some reason neither Francesca nor her brother were comfortable in Corigliano.

In this corner of the Salento there is an elongated triangle of three small towns, Sogliano, Cutrofiano and Corigliano. Sogliano and Cutrofiano, the home towns of Paola and Francesca, are close to each other, Corigliano is out on a limb. As outsiders there was no doubt where we felt most at home and at first we weren't sure why. Was it the lack of eating places in the first two? Was it the apparent lack of atmosphere in the same two? Was this, in turn, because these two were Jehovah's Witnesses' enclaves?

At the end of that evening we had spent in Porto Cesareo with Francesca and Ciccio, we left the doting couple in Leverano, where Ciccio lived, and headed back to Sogliano. Every town we went through seemed to have shut up for the night (it *was* well past midnight, after all) but we decided to head initially for Corigliano to see if Gino's was still open.

And it was. At almost one in the morning we were sitting outside Bar del Arco sipping an early morning coffee and nibbling at a few left-over *stuzzichini**. Nor were we alone, Corigliano still seemed to have plenty of life in it. Gino told us that he didn't expect to close until gone two … and he'd be open again at seven!

Another possible explanation was that Corigliano was one of the nine towns known collectively as La Grecia Salentina which claimed on-going links to the language, culture and traditions of their Greek origins. In subsequent visits to the Salento area we tried to visit all of these towns and it has to be said that we did feel they were in some way distinctive. It's something we found difficult to quantify, something almost imperceptible and elusive … on the other hand, we knew these towns were supposed to be 'different', so perhaps it's not surprising that we found them so. Maybe this 'difference' is just a load of old codswallop; it's just as likely that the inhabitants of Sogliano and Cutrofiano spurned the folks down the road in Corigliano because they were better at football or knitting! Who knows?

I think Gino should have the last word on this … when we tried to get out of him some sort of explanation for Corigliano being *particolare*, he did the Italian shoulder-shrug, synchronised with a slight pouting of the lips, smiled and said simply, '*A Corigliano, c'è sempre festa … sempre festa*'. And, we were to discover, he was right – it was always party-time in Corigliano d'Otranto, always something going on.

*Stuzzichini … a glorious word which we used to find difficult to say. We first came across these snacks or nibbles when we had lunch in Galatina the day we arrived. Many bars and cafés offer *stuzzichini* with drinks but in Apulia these have become almost an art form – wonderful miniature pieces of pizza and pastry bedecked or stuffed with all sorts of little goodies, olives, salami, peppers, pesto, tomatoes and flavours to take your breath away. In some places they are a meal in themselves and a small charge is made for a plate to share. The singular of *stuzzichini is stuzzichino* which is also the Italian word for 'tormentor' – this is no accident!

But first we had to get the football out of the way. England were playing Croatia and Francesca, a closet England fan, wanted to watch the game with us ... unfortunately Italian television was showing another game (Switzerland–France). I asked Gino if he knew of anywhere we could catch the match ... step forward Mr Fixit.

Surprise, surprise, Gino had a sort of mezzanine floor upstairs with a television that could pick up the satellite signal ... and he simply turned it over to the three of us and plied us with *stuzzichini* and beer. What a guy. What a result, England won 4–2.

The next night a poor Italian team was playing Bulgaria and we knew we ought to support Gino and his regulars and watch the game with them in the bar. To qualify for the knock-out round Italy needed to win convincingly *and* one of the other two teams in their group (Denmark or Sweden) needed to be well beaten. Neither happened. It was a night for national mourning as the Italian team headed instead for the airport and the next flight home.

We breakfasted at Gino's the following morning and shared again in these moments of national depression. Never had we seen so many grown men on the verge of tears as, philosophically, they knocked back their *espressi*, read and re-read their newspapers in the faint hope that it was all a huge mistake and shook their heads in disbelief. Over and over again the word *brutta* infiltrated their conversations; they were talking about the Italian team, *brutta* means 'ugly' and 'awful' and lots of other things in-between.

Just relieved that it hadn't been the England team that had dealt the fatal blow, we demonstrated our solidarity and shared in their pain ... and reminded them that this was only the European Cup, there was always the big one, the World Cup, in a couple of years. How prophetic that was!

We had come to the Salento because, on the map at least, there was, in every direction, something to do, somewhere to go. We were not disappointed. Other than Corigliano, the two places we tended to gravitate towards were Maglie*, where there were some interesting shops and an excellent *gelateria,* and Otranto, about twenty-five kilometres due east on the Mare Adriatico.

The road to Otranto is typical of the Salento, miles of perpetual flatness which eventually gives way to a more undulating landscape before winding down to the sea and into the ancient heart of this jewel of a town. Two things dominate Otranto: the blueness of the sea and the old town's labyrinth of *vicoli* encapsulated within the ancient city walls and touching both castle and sea.

We never tired of walking these narrow streets. Yes, they were inhabited mainly by purveyors of enticements for tourists but in among them there were shops and restaurants that serviced the needs of real people. Somehow these ancient edifices coped with this modest tourist onslaught; in Otranto it was the strong buildings, the ageing stone, the well-paved alleyways, the ancient doorways, the foot-worn steps, the dazzling sun and the seductive sea that we saw long before we noticed that there were other people wandering about in shorts and sporting cameras. People like us.

It is in the more modern beach-fronted Otranto that resident tourists mingle and munch and, yes, this part is fast becoming a typical holiday enclave for bums on beaches. But if it's not for you (and it certainly wasn't for us) then the old town remains a welcoming and timeless outpost.

---

*It was in one of Maglie's narrow alleyways that we came across the birthplace of the Italian politician Aldo Moro. His claim to fame should have been that he had been Itay's Prime Minister but in March 1978 he was taken by the so-called Red Brigades and held hostage for 55 days. The government refused to meet the demands of his kidnappers (a decision that still remains controversial in Italy) and Moro's body was found in the boot of a car in early May.

But Otranto has a past, a particularly bloody past which, at this time, we knew nothing about and bore no relation to the little town we knew and loved. It was the husband of one of Corigliano's several hairdressers that first broached the subject on a balmy evening when we were drinking at Gino's and acting as interpreter for a group of Turkish students ...

Forgive me for putting my own spin on this tale ... it seems that Otranto was one of those many places dotted around the Mediterranean where, in the past, East and West met and where religion and barbarism walked hand in hand to leave a legacy of confusion and hatred and of course, for the survivors, places of worship wherein to give thanks for having been delivered from the other sides's places of worship.

Nothing, it seems, changes, just gods and prophets, the apparent inspiration for the deeds and thoughts of many.

At the time of writing a 13- or 23-year girl or woman (some of the press seem to think that the age is important) has just been stoned to death for having accused some men of raping her. The men, guilty or innocent, and the circle of stoners will no doubt have spent a little time before and after, praying, facing this way or that or, in some other way, acknowledging that they are but the followers of this strand or that group of believers in something or someone who condones such actions.

It seems that, even in the 21st century, religious fervour and one of its subsets, barbarism, continue to walk hand in hand.

We decided to approach our first visit to the city of Lecce using a revolutionary new timing concept ... we aimed to arrive just after four in the afternoon, an hour or so before the end of the *siesta* and before the hordes returned to take up all those lovely empty parking spaces. It worked like a dream.

We parked up with ease on the ring-road side of the park and had a leisurely walk through it and into a city slowly returning to life. We had just enough time to explore and enjoy the sights of the city before the shutters went up and the shopkeepers, half-in, half-out of the doorways, relished a few more drags on that last cigarette and made one final, last-minute check that there were no messages on the *cellulare*.

For many people venturing into deepest Apulia, particularly by train, Lecce is as far as they get. They are drawn to La Firenza del Sud, the southern Florence, by the magnificent architecture that flaunts the warm pink of the local sandstone, a stone so easy to work that it remains one of Lecce's main exports. In among the grander façades are curving arches and delicate balustrades competing for your attention with open-to-the-world 'shops' where local craftsmen and women work in stone, wood, ceramics and glass. These are people who want to talk, who want to see you marvel at their skill and share in the pride that it gives them.

Not surprisingly, we are suckers for such chit-chat and not understanding eighty percent of what's being said never seems to deter us. Here, unlike Alberobello, we never felt any pressure not to leave empty-handed and when we did eventually buy a piece of glass it was because we wanted to and knew that it would remind us of a small side-street and a generous and skilled craftswoman on a warm evening in Lecce. And, even more importantly, it would remind us that it was here that we cocked a snook at the *siesta* and got our timing spot-on for the first time.

Though we were still staying at Paola's place in Sogliano, we had emotionally and mentally migrated to Corigliano d'Otranto, to such an extent that Francesca used to tease us about it; it sometimes felt almost as if we'd crossed the Rubicon and entered some strange forbidden land. Undaunted by such ridicule, we ate every night in a different restaurant here in a vain attempt to find a favourite – it was a futile task, we simply liked most of them for different reasons. For the first time, if pressed to choose to eat at our most favourite, Kay and I would have eaten separately and alone.

It turned out that Francesca had known all along about the variety of places to eat in Corigliano and she and her brother, her cousin, Rosella (and Rosella's boyfriend) and Paola (and her boyfriend) all joined us there for our final meal in the Salento. Francesca chose the venue, a small *pizzeria* that we'd missed but where she clearly had eaten before.

It was an enlightening evening. As ever, Francesca was *la traduttrice più importante*, the translater-in-chief; her brother, Salvatore, appeared to be in charge of embarrassing the waitresses with the glint in his eye and the sharpness of his wit; Paola, on the other hand, had one eye to her religion and the other on her watch lest she overstayed her welcome in the real world and turned into a pumpkin; and the wonderful Rosella quite rightly decided that it was her role in life to teach me all the 'naughty' words in Italian *and* then allow me to practise them!

Rosella's boyfriend was interesting too, he was on leave from his one-year National Service stint with the Italian forces in Afghanistan and was clearly enjoying the life. While soldiering alongside the UK forces in Kabul he had picked up a modicum of English which, curiously, seemed to include most of the words that Rosella was teaching me in Italian!

Our time was up in the Salento. We vacated Paola's house and said our goodbyes to her family before heading for Corigliano and more emotional goodbyes with Gino and his regulars. One of these, Nicola, was there with his wife, local hairdresser Isabella, and their young daughter, Mareka. Nicola explained that he would have liked to have talked to us more but that his English was not too good ... on the other hand his wife could speak French and maybe when (not 'if') we returned we might all get together again ...

We embraced Gino, all of his staff, Nicola, Isabella and Mareka (who said goodbye in perfect English) and headed for the main road north and my appointment with the Barber of Brindisi. En route we had much to think about, two weeks of people and places indelibly fixed in our minds and, most of all, a little *villetta* on the outskirts of Corigliano that we longed to stay in, sooner rather than later.

This, our second visit to Brindisi, involved no transgressions, well, not from us anyway. We knew where we were going, knew that there was no fourth set of traffic lights and easily found a place to park within five minutes walk of the Piazza Cairoli and *il lampo*. He remembered me and my hair and soon got to work on two week's growth, though this time he had Kay for an audience.

She was not disappointed ... I could see her wide-eyed, astonished reflection in the mirror and with it the realisation that I had not been exaggerating this guy's amazing take on a short, back and sides. Within minutes the deed was done and we were back in the sun sitting quietly watching the world go by and wondering how to spend our last few hours in Apulia when the muted bustle of a hot Saturday was interrupted by the loudest FUCK OFF! I had ever heard.

This English speaker was a high-heeled twenty-something blonde dressed in pink and trailing a pink suitcase-on-wheels. The object of her 'affection' was about ten metres nearer us, another twenty-something in jeans and tee-shirt, a small rucksack on his back and a clone-pink valise in one hand.

The latter he suddenly hurled towards his erstwhile companion with an endearing, "Well, you can fuck off too and carry your own fucking luggage for a change." As she stopped to reunite valise and suitcase, the guy did as he was bid and did indeed 'fuck off' in the general direction of the sea hotly pursued by a screaming and swearing pinkness fighting with her luggage and her heels to stay in an upright position.

A few Italian eyebrows were raised as they got the general flavour of what was going on; *il lampo* emerged from his salon to take stock of the situation. But, nosey to a fault, only Kay and I decided to do some follow-up work.

First of all, unlike the Pink Panted who had momentarily suspended swearing to adjust her footwear, we noticed that the man in her life had made a left up a side street about fifty metres down the Corso Umberto. We followed the PP and watched as she sped past the turning, still spouting loud expletives to no-one in particular. We turned left and, unknown to him, joined the fugitive for a cup of coffee in the sun while somewhere a few streets away the air was blue with pink.

He quickly downed his *espresso* and headed back towards Corso Umberto but went straight across and down another side street. We were about to follow when we became aware of the PP's dulcet tones approaching back up Corso Umberto and decided to wait and see what happened next. She trundled past us, blonde hair uncontrolled, arms and attached baggage flailing and, for the first time, we were really not sure what to do ... we knew where he'd gone but should we intercede and tell the PP? Would that be the right thing to do? Did we run the risk of her turning her wrath on us?

As we hesitated the moment had gone, she was heading back towards the Piazza Cairoli where it had all begun; perhaps he would do the same and they'd reunite, arms outstretched in a gleeful slow-motion embrace and all would be well with the world. And if that was not to be the scenario then, we wondered, who had the tickets for the next stage of their journey?

A couple of hours later we were back in Brindisi Airport queueing at the check-in on the last leg of our Apuglian adventure. It was a sad time, we liked this place so much that I was already rehearsing the words I would have to say on the phone to the email-less Gino in order to book a week with him in September.

In the corner of my eye a flash of pink momentarily interrupted my thoughts ... I turned round for a second or two and then whispered in Kay's ear ... "Don't look now, but guess who's got their tongue down who's throat and is going to be on the same flight as us?"

Gino's *villette* in the countryside and the passing traffic

Back to the Salento

When it came to phoning Gino to arrange accommodation for September, I cheated. Instead of doing it myself, I asked Ivano to make the call for me and that way I was sure that, on the appointed day at the appointed hour, Gino would be waiting for us at Brindisi Airport. He was.

Within the hour we were once again sitting in Bar del Arco having dropped off our bags at Gino's *villette* and returned to Corigliano with him. We were plied with wine, coffee and *stuzzichini* and, as Gino would be driving us back to into the country, I didn't have to watch my alcohol intake.

Gino picked us up at nine the next morning and took us to what seemed to be an up-market garage with subtle 'dodgy' undertones on the outskirts of Galatina where, we suspected, he was calling in a favour. The line of cars out front looked top notch, racy even, and I had mentally been behind the wheel of most by the time our car for the week appeared fresh from a pre-scrapyard limbo somewhere round the back. It was a less-than-youthful, whitish Fiat Tipo, a model that was discontinued in 1995.

Still, it's the thought that counts and Gino had got us a pre-power-steering-age bargain that was probably neither taxed nor insured. We signed some forms, promising to look after it for the week, made a quick inspection and, to save time, made a note of all the places where there *weren't* any scratches or dents.

No matter, we were mobile and we had a visit planned – to the shop in Cutrofiano where Francesca worked. Only problem was she didn't know we were in the country and we had a little surprise for her.

We parked up about ten metres from the shop and got out of the car; as we did so we could see a couple of women enter the shop. I called Francesca's cellphone which she answered almost immediately:

"Hi, is that Francesca?" I said, "This is Niall."

"Niall, Niall, what a surprise … it's really good to hear from you …

"How's Ciccio? I asked, deliberately prolonging the conversation, "And your mum and dad …?"

"Everyone's good … good … Niall, listen … can I call you back … the shop's a bit busy at the moment … I've got lots of people in the shop?"

As we talked, Kay and I were approaching the shop's large glass door.

"I know you've lots of customers in the shop … I saw them go in …"

"What did you say?" said a puzzled Francesca as we opened the door to the shop.

"I said I saw them go in …"

She raised her head when she realised she could hear me on her phone *and* in the shop. And she dropped everything, including her beloved cellphone, her *telefonino*, as she rushed to embrace us amid a cacophony of less-than-polite Italian expletives.

The expression on her face was priceless … it had been

worth the subterfuge, particularly as Francesca now had to explain to all her perplexed potential customers exactly what was going on. And when they had all left empty-handed she retrieved her cellphone from the counter and called Ciccio to bend his ear with the story.

Despite the shock to the system, she was really pleased to see us ... well, who wouldn't be? And any doubts were soon expelled when I finally bought that expensive Diesel watch I'd coveted since our last visit to the shop in June ... sadly the generous discount she gave me only cancelled out the unforeseen rise in price since then.

Thus began a whirlwind round of social engagements in and around Corigliano ... by the end of which we were close to exhaustion, laden with goodies and in dire need of a holiday.

With Francesca, Ciccio and Rosella we had another late night in Porto Cesareo to renew existing friendships and trample over old ground while, back in Corigliano, we were preparing to meet up again with Nicola, Isabella and Mareka.

Gino had spilt the beans and forewarned Nicola of our return visit and, instead of beating a hasty retreat north, south, east or west, he and Isabella soon caught up with us in Bar del Arco and invited us round for *il pranzo*, a lunchtime nibble the next day.

What we hadn't expected was *la nonna* (Isabella's mother) and her *sorella* (sister) Elena and her *marito* (husband) Enzo, who had made the trip up from Gallipoli for the occasion; Mareka had also invited the ever-beaming Marco, though we were never sure whether he was friend or family, or even whether it mattered.

Following on from a (very deliberate) 'just-in-case-you-were-thinking-about-it-but-actually-we're-not-such-big-horse-eaters' chat the night before, the conversation evolved into the paucity of chicken dishes on most Italian menus. I think Isabella took this as a hint and by the time we stepped out into the small enclosed patio-garden behind her hairdressing salon most of the *galline* in the immediate area appeared to have been culled, plucked and cooked!

The generosity of our hosts and their family was almost beyond words; the plentiful food was brought to the table in that nonchalant Italian way which makes everything look simple and sophisticated at the same time. As the wine flowed, potential language problems seemed to evaporate and even *la nonna,* realising we weren't from Mars, stopped scrutinising us and joined in with the general merriment that soon echoed round the neighbourhood ... punctuated only by the silence that accompanied the concentrated effort needed to down the cream-laden *torta* that was our contribution to the proceedings.

Along with some of Nicola's home-made wine, we staggered back to the car with a huge bottle of Elena and Enzo's *capperi* (capers) that had come straight from their garden in Gallipoli ... to where we were invited to come and pick our own some time.

To this day we're not sure how it was that we four got on (and Mareka makes five) but get on we did. I sometimes wonder whether it's the *lack* of language that facilitates such friendships ... perhaps if we could communicate more fluently in each other's tongue and talk about the things that really make people tick – politics, religion and the like – then maybe we wouldn't get on at all.

That said, I can't imagine *anyone* not getting along with Gino!

We saw Francesca and Ciccio a couple of times but nothing of Francesca's mother and father who did not approve of their relationship. Ciccio was divorced and had two children and Francesca's mother in particular was being more than a little frosty which made living at home a little difficult for her.

They were desperate to get away and spend some real time together so we suggested that they come to Bath and stay with us for a while – which they did two months later. It was to be their first holiday together.

Our week came and went. In between the socialising we sat out in the sun in Gino's garden, breakfasted in his bar and popped in of an evening as well; we re-acquainted ourselves with a *gelato* or two in Otranto and started on our tour of the nine towns of La Grecia Salentina; we ate again at the Borgo Antico in Galatina and still failed to find 'our' restaurant in Corigliano. But we did manage to narrow it down to two – the one with the best *antipasti* (which I liked) and the one with the most varied menu (which Kay preferred). We compromised and ate alternately at each and then tried a third, a pizzeria, with Nicola and Isabella.

We also made a new friend. His name was Guiseppe and on most days he worked Gino's land next to our *villetta*. He was of indeterminate age, somewhere between seventy-five and eighty-five, and sported a single tooth. Despite the language barrier – older people, we discovered, rarely made any allowances for the fact that you might not understand them and pressed on regardless, teeth or no teeth – we had many an interesting chat with Guiseppe, usually about the vegetables he was planting, watering or harvesting. Before we left we bought him a couple of bottles of his favourite beer ... and in so doing cemented a friendship that was, for me at least, to have unpredictable repercussions.

On one occasion Guiseppe was bad-mouthing someone whose car he recognised passing down the lane in front of the *ortocello,* the allotment; we didn't really get the essence of his distaste until he made a particular hand-gesture which we knew to be a shorthand for saying that this was a 'bad' person. In such cases 'bad' normally meant one word, mafia.*

All too soon it was our last day. Gino picked us up on a sunny, late-September afternoon and took us to the airport via a last drink at the Bar del Arco. As we turned our backs on our trusty scrapyard-bound jalopy still parked outside his *villetta*, we knew that we'd be back here soon.

And at Brindisi Aeroporto, when we said our final goodbyes to Gino and I glimpsed a solitary tear in his eye, I knew that we'd always be made very welcome in this part of Apulia.

Unknown to Kay, Gino already had the projected dates in his pocket.

Although mafia-type organisations are normally associated with three areas of southern Italy – Sicily, Calabria (the 'ndrangheta) and the Naples area (the camorra) – Apulia clearly felt left out and in the late 1970s a similar criminal organisation was formed and duly gave itself a long-winded, and instantly forgettable name: sacra corona unita (united sacred crown).

First stop Naples

We planned to return to Corigliano the following June but this time we were taking a three-week holiday *and* we were going to fly from Bristol.

We both hated that drive between Bath and Stansted via the M25 and so, when easyJet announced their new route from Bristol to Rome, we just had to sign up for it. We knew that from Rome it was a six-hour drive down to Apulia but it was six hours on the much quieter Italian roads and we didn't have to do it all at once. There were places en route we wanted to visit like Naples, Vesuvius, Pompeii and Herculanium.

The plan was that we would fly to Rome Ciampino, stay one night in a hotel next to the airport then head down to the high central spine of the Sorrento peninsula and stay two days in an apartment in Sant'Agata sui Due Golfi before heading for Corigliano for two weeks and then back to the same apartment in Sant'Agata for our last three days.

For all sorts of reasons this was to be a holiday we would never forget ... and it all started on the tarmac at Bristol.

Just as we were about to push back from the terminal, the pilot announced that there was a problem at Ciampino which would delay our take-off for about ten minutes. Ten minutes

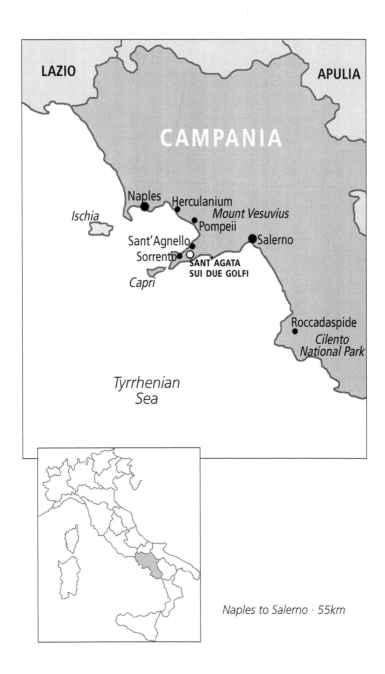

LAZIO

APULIA

CAMPANIA

Naples

Herculanium

Mount Vesuvius

Ischia

Pompeii

Sant'Agnello

Salerno

Sorrento

**SANT AGATA
SUI DUE GOLFI**

Capri

Roccadaspide

*Cilento
National Park*

*Tyrrhenian
Sea*

Naples to Salerno · 55km

later and we were heading for the runway when the plane pulled over onto the apron and stopped once more.

The pilot announced a further problem at Ciampino and we waited. Twenty minutes later he confirmed that we couldn't land at Ciampino but that he had managed to get clearance to head for Rome's other, much larger, intercontinental airport, Fiumicino. He then gave everyone ten minutes on their mobiles to change any arrangements at the Rome end.

And now for the easyJet advert ... budget airlines get a lot of stick but I think easyJet did us all proud that day; they got everyone to Rome, albeit to another airport, and they also gave us an opportunity to make alternative arrangements. For us that meant one call ... to Hertz at Ciampino to ask them to change our car pick-up to Fiumicino. We'd just get to the hotel a little later than planned.

And get there we did, and only about an hour and a half late. We were tired and needed a drink. I asked the receptionist-cum-barman for two glasses of red wine ... he took one look at our jaded jowls, reached for two tumblers from the shelf, opened a bottle of wine and poured half into each glass. He could obviously read our minds!

Next morning and we were back in the glorious Italian sun and heading south towards Naples and Sant'Agata sui Due Golfi. But before we got to Sant'Agata we had a rendezvous with a volcano, the infamous destroyer of Pompeii, Mount Vesuvius.

Though by no means as impressive as Etna, it stands alone for what it did in August 79CE to the coastal towns along the Bay of Naples, most notably to Herculanium and Pompeii, both of which we planned to visit on our return trip from Apulia.

I managed to take two impressive photos here, both of the

Human traffic only in Naples' *centro storico*

erupting Vesuvius one of which was from the air. Of course they were of postcards on the rack outside the souvenir shop but were in among genuine shots of the enormous summit crater and fooled more than a few people both in Italy and in the UK ... though I would have thought that the one from the air was a bit of a giveaway.

We arrived in Sant'Agata, high up atop the Sorrento peninsula, late in the afternoon and, as arranged, called our host, Carlo, who appeared a few minutes later to guide us to his exquisite home, Villa Belvedere, and our top-storey apartment.

Sant'Agata sui Due Golfi gets its extended name from its elevated position overlooking two different seas, the Golfo di Napoli to the north and the Golfo di Salerno to the south; our apartment at Villa Belvedere offered spectacular views over the latter.

On the northern coastline of the peninsula, overlooking the Bay of Naples, there is a railway linking Sorrento with Naples and that's where we headed the next morning to catch the train from Sant'Agnello to Naples and an experience that has no equal anywhere in Italy.

I suppose we should have been prepared for something different. On the previous day, as we innocently circum-navigated Naples' urban sprawl on the *autostrada,* we both picked up on a disconcerting disorder as we negotiated the endless roadworks: it seemed that many drivers decided that this was their opportunity to put in a practice lap for the Italian Grand Prix. We shrugged our shoulders, Italian-style, and put it down to experience ... perhaps word had got out that the Ferrari team were on the lookout for a new driver.

One word sums up Naples – volatile. Everything about this place speaks of life on an explosive edge.

Amid a backdrop of an astonishing ramshackle of architecture and colours, there are countless *vicoli* with shops and workshops edging ever closer towards the hordes of people trying to press their way through from one street to another. Exaltations to look at this or buy that do battle with scooters that just press on regardless as they jostle for pole position within this mesmerising anarchy.

Ever present are the inflections of raised voices and the frenetic waving of arms, the mushrooming swirls of cigarette smoke and the endless tuneless cellphones, their intrusive ring always interrupted by the same word ... *pronto?* If *chuiso* is the most common written word in Italian, then *pronto?* is surely the one uttered most often.

And always there in the background are the glorious aromas of fresh coffee and food, enveloping invitations that swirl insidiously out into the streets, that weave and wave until it is all but impossible not to succumb.

Naples attacks and tempts the senses. Every sense. This is the place for people-watchers; a place to find a kerbside café from which to sit and stare and wonder who all these people are, what it is they do and where they go at night (if they ever make it!).

We found such a place but our mental gymnastics were abruptly curtailed when we realised that we were privy to a strange phenomenon ... the colour blindness that seems to have afflicted so many here.

True, it doesn't seem to affect people on foot so much ... their stylish attire is still colour co-ordinated, they can still recognise the colours of a Neapolitan ice-cream and certainly they don't seem to have any problem with the banknotes. No, this affliction only seems to have ravaged the senses of those who get behind the wheel of a car or, worse still, behind the handlebars of a *motorino*, a scooter.

It's a simple affliction which appears to have no known cure hereabouts; it's an inability to recognise the difference between red, amber and green traffic lights. In Naples, whatever their colour, most drivers seem to think they are stuck on green!

The traffic in Naples is truly mechanised mayhem. The man or woman behind every wheel appears to have one objective: to blindly get there first!

If it were just a race, the goal, the winning post, would be known to everyone taking part; on the streets of Naples there are as many destinations as there are cars and scooters and their drivers *all* want to be 'somewhere' before anyone else.

This is driving with the gloves off, focused driving that relies on ruthless and rule-less instinct and, yes, there was a side of me that had a sneaking admiration for the winding and the weaving, the near misses, the screeching brakes, the squeezing in and the pulling out, the sudden turns, the cacophony of horns, the frenzied gesticulations, the revving up in anticipation ...

As a seasoned Italian driver I have to confess that I was itching to have a go; I was curious to see if my skill at fairground dodgems would translate into this real-life, no-holds-barred chaos. But I suppose I realised that, were I out there, I might have felt obliged to stop at the occasional red light or I would have spoilt this mercurial ballet by signalling before pulling out or changing lanes ... the sort of thing that, in Naples, could cause an accident.

And so it remains an unfulfilled ambition, along with naked skydiving and picnicking in Baghdad, some day I would like to drive around Naples.

Even as our train trundled back round the coast to Sant'Agnello, the sights and sounds of Naples continued to dominate our thoughts. But gradually, as the city receded and we looked out across the shimmering curve of the bay, I was reminded of my other motive for being here.

As a teenager I spent many of my summers in the towns in and around Killiney Bay, south of Dublin, and remember being told that the vista and ambience here were akin to the Bay of Naples, indeed many local people actually called it the Bay of Naples. At the time I had no idea where the Bay of Naples was nor that one day I might find myself there with a unique opportunity to compare and contrast ... and, what's more, from a bay-side train which is something else both places have in common.

Spectacularly beautiful though Killiney Bay is, this is no real contest ... it's like suggesting that the centre of Paris and the seafront of Blackpool are similar because they've both got towers!

Driving us mad

While driving in Naples may well be a unique experience, driving in Italy can best be described as an 'interesting' experience.

As you may recall, on our very first evening there we had to negotiate the hilltop town of Monterchi, temporarily snarled-up by the swarms of people attracted to the local Polenta Festival. It was a baptism by fire, particularly as we didn't really know what was happening, we didn't have any language, we assumed that the uniformed guy waving at us was a policeman, it was dark and we were very tired.

Somehow we survived this encounter and emerged unscathed on the other side of town. In the UK there would probably have been signs indicating what was happening and suggesting a diversion; drivers would have been encouraged to form an orderly queue.

Similarly when we first arrived in Brindisi we found ourselves driving down a pedestrianised street, in the left-hand carriageway and right behind a police car doing the same; a few minutes later we arrived at our destination by following directions the wrong way down a one-way street.

In trying to isolate, analyse and explain the idiosyncrasies that become the Italian driving experience, there are inevitable generalisations based on personal experience. Over the years, as I have become indoctrinated, I am aware that my viewpoint has shifted and that there is now much of the Italian driver in me … though only in Italy, I hasten to add.

As I write, I am aware that in less than two weeks I will once again be driving there. I know that as soon as I get behind that wheel and mentally switch to driving on the right, I will change; I will not lose my basic instinct to get where I'm going safely but I will not be driving in the same way that I did a couple of hours earlier en route to the airport.

It is almost impossible to explain the difference, the best I can do is to describe it as a reaction to being part of a different driving environment. When I was a newcomer to Italy I was reacting to this different experience as someone fresh from England would; now I react with experience of and empathy with the Italian environment. In all the years I've been driving in Italy, I cannot recall ever having seen a road accident; that said, over the same time, I've rarely seen a car without dents and scratches but, I suspect, most of these will have been self-inflicted, the result of erratic manoeuvring or careless reversing.

Of course there *are* road accidents, as evidenced by the occasional roadside floral tributes to the victims, and it would seem that many of these have something in common – they are on or near a bend. For some reason many Italian drivers have an uncontrollable urge to overtake approaching a bend in the road, a bend they cannot possibly see around, a bend towards which another car may be fast approaching. And yet they take the risk and ninety-nine times out of a hundred it pays off or they just make it; clearly sometimes they don't.

So what is it that characterises Italian driving? What is it that makes it such a different driving experience?

First of all my experiences may not be typical of all Italy. I have done most of my driving south of Rome and on Sicily and Sardinia. Maybe these areas are themselves unique – maybe not.

If there is indeed a geographic element that characterises *my* Italian driving experience then I suspect it has an historical element and is linked to the time and the rate at which the car became the standard mode of transport in southern Italy.

A quarter of a century ago in the rural south the car took second place to the three-wheels of the multifarious manifestations of the wondrous *Apè*, the workhorse of both the land and the town. For many here the car was but an extension of the *Apè* ... a bit bigger, a bit better, a bit more classy but nonetheless essentially a vehicle for moving things and people around. That's why it is not unusual to see half a wardrobe sticking out of the side (not the back) of a car, or a ladder sticking out of the roof doubling the height of the car or a pick-up with a load of furniture and boxes and a young lad swinging left to right trying to hold it all down.

In an effort to incorporate some sort of order to what I have experienced I'm going to go out on a limb and try to categorise some of my observations ... at which point I should apologise for the crime of generalisation melded with a smattering of personal experience. Nonetheless, apologies already forgotten, what follows *is* normal and, I have to confess, I have become one of these people (but more of that later). So here goes ...

Hooting

The horn is an essential part of the Italian driving experience. In England it is normally a warning signal while the stereotypical Italian is supposed to sound it as a demonstration of his or her (Latin) impatience when in a traffic jam.

Not so.

Firstly (and most often) it is a sign of recognition ... for the Italian driver it is a way of saying 'hello', a way of acknowledging that he or she has passed a friend, a relative, an acquaintance or an out-the-corner-of-the-eye-half-recognised vehicle; believe it or not, it is also a way of saying 'thank you' when somebody does something courteous or helpful.

Frequently in smaller towns (as opposed to cities where indeed it can be a reflection of frustration) it is a sound associated with the door-to-door purveyors of the essentials of life: it could be the bread man, the fish man, the cheese man, the butcher, the fruit-and-veg man, the clothes man, the pots and pan man, the soft-furnishings man, the cleaning utensils man, the knife sharpening man ... ten different horns ... or maybe even a dozen or more if there are two bread men and three fruit-and-veg men! Locals *do* actually know which is which *and* whose horn they prefer when it comes to buying bread.

Finally, there is the cacophony of horns that accompany the cavalcade of cars going to and from a wedding. The first time you encounter this you think the world has gone mad ... it has!

Parking

In days of yore the Great British Public was indoctrinated into the art of parking by television adverts that demonstrated how to reverse into a convenient space between two other cars. These adverts never reached Italy.

When we stayed in Sciacca our Sicilian host shared with me his thoughts on the art of driving in Italy; he said: "You will never really drive like an Italian until you learn to park like an Italian." I looked at him knowingly and in unison we said the same word ... ANYWHERE!

Where to begin? There are so many examples that spring to mind ... some of which I have even done myself (but I'd be too embarrassed to say which).

It's all about the need to solve a short-term parking problem. In the UK if there's no obvious space you keep driving till you find one or you decide not to pop into that shop after all, maybe another day; the Italian driver does not necessarily see the lack of a car-length space as a major impediment. For example ...

There is just about a car length between two cars but not enough to reverse into the space ... drive into it diagonally and leave the car's rear end sticking out; or drive into it diagonally and put the front end on the footpath; better still, a bit of both.

Your mobile phone rings or you spot something worth photographing as you approach a roundabout or a hairpin bend ... drive onto the roundabout or the bend, park up and take the call or reach for the camera.

You want to park outside a particular shop but there is no space ... double park as close to the shop as possible.

You want to park outside a particular shop but there is no space and to double park would mean that oncoming traffic might have difficulty in passing ... double park anyway.

You want to park outside a particular shop but there is no space and someone has got there first and has double parked outside it ... double park behind or treble park.

You want to park outside a particular shop but there is no space on either side of the road ... park in the middle of the road.

The only space near your favourite shop is by a pedestrian crossing ... park on the pedestrian crossing.

You see the local fruit and veg man's van parked up in a busy street and remember you're short of potatoes ... double park alongside him.

You see a parking space down a quiet one-way street but you are at the wrong end ... drive down the street, make a three-point turn and park up.

You are at the supermarket but only want a couple of things ... forget about all those parking bays and just park outside the main entrance.

You want to park at the supermarket in your brand-new car and don't want to get it scratched by the careless parking of others ... park in the middle of two parking bays or, better still, atop the 'cross' of four bays.

In (southern) Italy it is generally accepted that people park for a purpose and that it is usually a short-term purpose. None of the above resulted in Armageddon, none of them hurt anybody, none of them really disrupted traffic for any length of time ... they all solved a transitory need and in most cases nobody was any the wiser.

And if someone says to you, "You can't park there", it's probably not true ... they might well just be keeping the space free for a friend or a family member.

In the interests of balance, all of the above needs to be put in context. In many larger towns and cities there are parking restrictions whether or not you are parked at an angle half up on the pavement; these involve buying a ticket from a machine or a scratch card, usually from a *tabaccheria*, for display inside the car. Where these restrictions exist they are, as we were to discover, well policed but, depending on the normal shopping hours locally, often only apply up to one o'clock and after four-thirty.

In addition there are places where you can park free for, say, half an hour and for these most hire cars have a disk in the window which is rotated to indicate the time of arrival.

Overtaking
In the UK the urge to overtake is generally confined to dual carriageways and motorways, indeed there are probably

many drivers who have never passed another (moving) vehicle other than on such roads.

In Italy, on the other hand, the same 'rule' applies to all roads, including winding rural roads, roads in towns and cities and the so-called *superstrada** ... if you want to go faster than the car in front, then you have to overtake it.

I have already alluded to the apparent urge to do so approaching bends (and the occasional fatal results of such recklessness) but on the whole the Italian driver is quite adept at weaving in and out unscathed and at no risk to others.

So 'natural' is the instinct to overtake that it is not unusual to be passed by a car which almost immediately turns off the road to left or right and you are left to wonder what the point was.

But, as ever, the Italians do things with panache and it is not unknown, on a *superstrada* for example, to be passed by a car which, in turn, is being passed by another car ... three cars all going in the same direction in a line across the highway. The triple by-pass ... enough to give you a heart attack.

Chatting

Italians are a gregarious people and friends and family are important so, when they're driving along and pass a friend or relative, either approaching or parked up, then it would be impolite not to stop alongside and exchange a word or two ... this doesn't seem to bother other drivers who have probably done the same themselves ... so they just drive round such impromptu encounters.

---

*Despite its grand name, the *superstrada* is no more than an important highway; it may be a dual carriageway, it may be peppered with odd bits of dual carriageway but, as for example the SS107 between the major centres of Cosenza and Crotone in Calabria, it is just as likely to be a wide-ish single carriageway in both directions with an additional metre-wide hard shoulder which you are expected to drift into when being overtaken.

For me, driving in Italy has been, on the whole, an enlightening experience. Now that I understand the rationale I find that to join in is infinitely more rewarding than criticising or pooh-poohing. I remember the first time I stopped alongside another car to speak to someone I knew, it was a milestone, it made me feel Italian and I knew that the driver behind would give me a bit of leeway to finish my conversation. ... as, indeed, I would have given him or her.

Let DH Lawrence have the last word on this. Writing in 1921 in *Sea and Sardinia* and speaking specifically about the drivers of southern Italy, he said, "I always have a profound admiration for their driving – whether of a great omnibus or a motor-car. It all seems so easy, as if the man were part of the car. ... A car behaves like a smooth, live thing, sensibly."

Back to Apulia

The magic and the mayhem of Naples still assaulting our senses, we bade temporary farewell to Sant'Agata sui Due Golfi; we would be back at Villa Belvedere in a couple of weeks for another few days before returning to Ciampino and Bristol. Apulia and a fortnight of peace and quiet in the sun beckoned.

We headed for the main *autostrada* south before cutting across country to Bari (on the east coast) and then south to Brindisi and on to Corigliano d'Otranto where we dropped in on Gino at Bar del Arco around mid-afternoon, some six hour later. All we wanted were the keys to the *villetta* but the Italian welcome is rarely a short affair and it was another hour before we finally started to unpack in our own little quiet corner of the Salento.

Work-wise it had been a hard year for both of us and we had been looking forward to relaxing here and doing almost nothing for two weeks before we headed back to the Sorrento Peninsula.

We hadn't given Francesca our exact date and time of arrival but we weren't planning any surprises this time and so the next day I gave her a call and we arranged to meet for lunch in Cutrofiano. As ever the welcome was effusive and we arranged to go out together for a meal with Ciccio and perhaps his children a couple of days later and to meet up with them sometime in Leverano, west of Lecce, where they were moving in to a new apartment in a little over a week.

And so it was we were initiated into an aspect of the Italian psyche to which we subsequently attached the self-explanatory, albeit long-winded, label, 'It's never quite what you expect'.

We had both thought that our arrangement with Francesca was quite simple: we would all get together for something to eat in a day or two. What we didn't expect was a call the same afternoon, no more than an hour or so after we'd seen each other, suggesting, almost insisting, that we went out together for a pizza that evening. I was not best pleased and soon became the villain of the piece.

We were tired, very tired, and all we wanted to do was sit in the sun and have a few drinks at Gino's for a couple of days. We certainly didn't want to socialise every night, particularly long-distance socialising, for two weeks, we just didn't have the energy. So I told Francesca that we would prefer to stick to our original arrangement and that I'd get back to her in a day or two to finalise things.

I could tell she wasn't happy but couldn't work out why she should not respect the space we needed for these next few days. I thought I explained it quite simply and sympathetically. All I could think of was that she had spent too long in London for in many ways I think her possessiveness (for that is what it appeared to be) was very un-Italian.

It bothered me, all the more so when, when we did meet up, I could tell that she was still not her usual bubbly self around us ... probably more 'me' than 'us'. I tried again to explain how tired we were and that, yes, we did want to see her and Ciccio but we weren't up to a string of late nights.

We did see them again a couple of times, on the last occasion to visit their smart new apartment in Leverano and to take them a house-warming present. Nevertheless, what had happened on that first day was a watershed and things were never quite the same between the three of us again. I exclude Ciccio as I'm not sure he was bothered one way or the other as his lack of English often seemed to exclude him anyway.

We had been visiting Italy for almost the same length of time that Francesca had lived in London and in that time I think she had absorbed the hustle and bustle of the London 'scene' while we had gone the other way and become more laid-back, more Italian. It's never quite what you expect.

A shadow was thus cast over our relationship and, albeit to a lesser extent, our holiday. Undaunted we did the usual things we liked doing ... we went to Otranto, we sat in the sun, we met up with Nicola and family, we sat in the sun, we visited some more of the 'Greek' towns, we sat in the sun ... and we visited the ports of Gallipoli* and Taranto for the first time.

We had actually driven to Gallipoli once before, on Francesca's recommendation, on our first visit to the Salento the previous summer ... unfortunately on that particular evening we got caught up in the traffic mayhem associated with yet another festival and just couldn't seem to find anywhere to park. So this second foray over to the Salento's western coast was bolstered by my new-found understanding that there was no such thing as not being able to find somewhere to park.

Being on the west coast, Gallipoli ('beautiful town' in Greek) overlooks the *Mare Jonica*, the Ionian Sea. The modern urban sprawl that is the initial welcome is less than 'beautiful' but

*Not to be confused with the Gallipoli peninsula in Turkey and the famous (and ultimately futile) First World War campaign which cost the lives of over 130,000 combatants on both sides.

soon gives way to its *raison d'être*, a picturesque fortified town on an island linked to the mainland by a narrow bridge dominated on its southern side by the imposing battlements of the fortress. We decided to drive across and round the one-way system and back to the mainland before parking up and doing the whole thing all over again on foot.

We walked around the outer edge of the island basking in its glorious sea-vistas, particularly of the tall Ostuni-white lighthouse on the nearby island of San Andrea, and the array of marinas, including the small fishing harbour that, like so many in this part of Italy, now casts an eye to the potential of the tourist industry. When something caught our attention, we made sorties in and out of the narrow *vicoli* punctuated by an assortment of *piazze* of multifarious sizes and importance.

In one, we stopped for a break and, as we sat sipping our mid-afternoon (non-alcoholic) cocktail, I tried to picture the scene here the previous year when, if the number of cars was anything to go by, this place would have been heaving. And, as ever on such occasions, the market stalls and the purveyors of all sorts of culinary delights would have been in their element; the sounds, the sights and the smells a heady mix as old and young greeted, chatted, tasted, laughed, smoked, drank and relaxed as they and this little island paradise were bathed in the last golden rays of the setting sun.

I think it was here in Gallipoli that I realised that, in Italy, I was definitely a night person. I recalled similar evenings in Corigliano, Galatina, Porto Cesareo, Alghero, Castellammare del Golfo and Siracusa, especially Siracusa, when the late evening heat, the hubbub of post-*siesta* humanity and the smell of jasmine and coffee mingled to create something uniquely Italian and singularly intoxicating.

If the northern European parking psyche hadn't kicked in a year ago I might have been able to add Gallipoli to that list … perhaps one day.

A couple of days later we decided to see what Porto Cesareo had to offer in the daytime ... we'd only ever been in the late evening with Francesca and Ciccio for a *gelato* when it was clearly a magnet for the young. We soon decided we preferred it at night and headed on further north along the winding road that hugged the coast all the way to the port of Taranto, the largest urban sprawl in this part of Apulia (indeed the third largest in southern Italy) and home to a significant part of the Italian Navy.

We knew we would be arriving at the start of the *siesta* but on this occasion it wasn't a problem as we weren't in shopping mode; all we wanted to do was walk by the harbours and the Citta Vecchia, the old town and have something to eat. Also on the itinerary was something less tangible, to try to equate 21st century Taranto with the place of culture it once was: as the Spartan town of Taras, lauded by Horace as his dearest nook on earth, 'where heaven grants a long springtime and warmth in winter', an erstwhile centre of ancient art specialising in ceramics and the birthplace of Aristoxenus who is credited with having been the first to notate 'western' music.

Like Siracusa and Gallipoli, Taranto's Citta Vecchia is an island; it differs in that there is mainland at both ends of the island. There is also a bridge at either end ... the most southerly of which, Il Ponte Girevole, a swing bridge, we crossed en route from the modern commercial and shopping part of the city. The northern bridge, crosses into the industrial heartland of Taranto*, originally based on its dockyards and related steel industry, and beyond towards the main arteries north to Potenza and Rome and west and south to Basilicata and Calabria.

We had read that the old city was known as much for its pickpockets and car thieves as for its architecture and

*These days Taranto is just as well known for its industrial legacy as it was once was for its culture. Its most recent claim to fame is as the most polluted city in Western Europe; also in 2006 it was officially declared bankrupt.

A grand *palazzo* in Taranto that has seen better days ... and perhaps will again

ambience. Like us, the pickpockets and car thieves were on holiday that day (as I had guessed they might be) and we enjoyed both the architecture and the ambience and, as it was early afternoon, we had the whole place almost to ourselves ... apart from one or two long-retired horse-and-cart thieves seeking a bit of shade.

It seemed as if life had stood still here for nigh on a thousand years. The buildings stood tall and proud without such a sense of decay that was so noticeable in parts of Siracusa. Some of the finer buildings are the old *palazzi* that were originally the residences of Taranto's aristocratic families. We explored the labyrinthine network of *vicoli* many of which led inexorably to the Via del Duomo that runs up the centre of the island. But there are *vicoli* and *vicoli* ... there are *vicoli* with arches, *vicoli* with stone steps, *vicoli* with tunnels, *vicoli* with dead ends and Taranto had them all, including the narrowest we'd ever seen. Here too we discovered the lengths that people will go to just to get their car as close to home as possible ... they turned up in the most unlikely places and with no obvious means of egress until, that is, you noticed the paint marks on the stone and the stone marks on the wing mirrors.

Although we walked by the castle and stopped to take a look at the Greek temple ruins (dating from the 6th century BCE) in the Piazza del Castello, it was the countless alleyways off the beaten track that took our breath away. As we were heading back to the car, the mass of humanity that called these narrow little streets 'home' was just beginning to wake up; Taranta's Citta Vecchia was slowly coming back to life just as it had done for hundreds of years.

Apart from our trips to Gallipoli and Taranto we didn't venture far from Corigliano. Gino's *villetta* and Corigliano d'Otranto itself were good bases and we were happy to do as little as possible. We also saw more of Guiseppe and his tooth this time; it was June, it was hot and there was more to do on the land and Guiseppe was happy to take a break every now and then for a chat ... until, that is, he sensed that Gino was just around the corner.

Almost every morning we found a little box of vegetables on the table outside our door ... a lettuce, a couple of tomatoes, some beans, a green pepper. Gradually the boxes got bigger as did the amount of fresh fare that Guiseppe was giving us until one day, one fateful day, he left us a loaf of bread as well.

Every day when we thanked him for his kindness he would shrug his shoulders and say, *di niente*, it's nothing; but on this particular day he went on to tell us that his wife had made the bread for us. We were even more humbled that a woman whom we'd never met should have gone to such trouble.

We were both looking forward to lunch. The table outside on the verandah was set. We had fresh vegetables and fruit, some cheese, a glass of red wine and, pride of place, a loaf of Apulian bread made especially for us ... I remember thinking how hard it must be for Guiseppe to eat such fine fare with that solitary tooth, especially the bread.

It's funny how a fleeting moment can change something in your life ... to date that first slice of Guiseppe's wife's bread has cost me around £2500.

I heard the sound of the break but wasn't sure what it was at first. I chewed a bit more before my tongue found the gap and I realised that I'd lost a tooth but knew that it was in fact a crown right at the front. Slowly I swallowed the bread, my tongue all the time searching for the tooth to make sure I didn't swallow it too. I found it, spat it out and quickly found a mirror to survey the damage to that enigmatic smile.

The peg of the crown was still attached to the tooth so I was able replace it and it seemed to fit snugly enough but dropped out again as soon as I loosened my hold. I immediately called my dentist in Bath and made an appointment for the day after we got back.

That evening, before we ate, we called into Gino's for an *aperitivo* and I showed him the damage (I omitted to mention Guiseppe's bread) and asked about the local dentist. As ever Mr Fixit was at hand and within seconds I was pointed in the right direction clutching one of Gino's business cards with the name of the dentist's nurse scribbled on the back.

Less than five minutes later I was sitting in the waiting room with about half a dozen others though I was the only one swatting up all the relevant words in the 'At the Dentist' section of my phrase book ... the most important one being *dottore* as dentists in Italy are always referred to as doctors and it is polite to use the title when addressing them.

I think that my fellow patients must have spilled the beans for when my turn came, *il dottore*, his nurse and another assistant had an expectant air about them as I was ushered into an ultra-modern surgery complete with hi-tech chair. I tried to explain what had happened – *il mia capsula è rotta* (my crown is broken) – and showed them the damage. I also tried to make some sort of conversation by mentioning Gino and that we were staying in the country, *in compagna*. I obviously got all that wrong as I heard the assistant whisper to the nurse that she thought I was actually from Campania, probably Naples ... as if that explained my lack of language and the appalling accent; I corrected this misunderstanding and explained that I was English-speaking and in Corigliano on holiday ... at least I think that's what I said.

It didn't take long for the crown to be glued back in place but I could see that *il dottore* wasn't a hundred percent certain that it would last – I got the impression that there could be another problem but it was only an impression, my Italian wasn't good enough to understand the details. The deed done I thanked everyone and tried to pay but instead was ushered out with a firm *di niente*. Two minutes later I was back at Gino's, where I once again showed off my enigmatic smile to Kay.

We had only a few days left in Corigliano, just enough time to have dinner with Gino and his wife at their home, to see Francesca and Ciccio one last time and then lunch the next day with Nicola, Isabella and Mareka and their extended family. On our last morning, just before we headed off on the long drive north to Sant'Agata sui Due Golfi and our return visit to Villa Belvedere, we had two final farewells to get out of the way.

We popped in to see the dentist and gave him and his colleagues a huge tray of mouth-watering pastries from the local *pasticceria*, much to the amusement of those sitting in the waiting room and the puzzlement of the woman *il dottore* abandoned in the chair, mid-treatment, while he came out to accept his payment in kind; it was the least we could do to repay such kindness.*

We also had to call in at Bar d'Arco to say our farewells to Gino and his regulars and to drop a hint that we would probably be back in September. As we embraced I knew I had been right about that tear I saw in his eye the previous September when he had taken us back to Brindisi airport ... this time he wept openly.

---

*When I saw my dentist in Bath the following week he checked over everything and told me that, as I'd heard a crack, it was likely that the root had split in which case the 'repair' wouldn't last. He was right and it was probably this that *il dottore* in Corigliano had been trying to explain to me. I deliberately didn't tell my dentist about the unusual payment method until the time came to pay *him* ... I asked if he wanted cash or cakes. Not surprisingly he looked puzzled until I explained how we'd paid *il dottore* in Apulia; he thought for a moment and said that cakes would be fine, it would make a pleasant change. So, next day I dropped off a tray of cakes at the surgery. Sadly, the subsequent treatment which, at the time of writing, has just been completed, has had to be paid for in the old-fashioned way.

A day and a half

The highlight of our second sojourn at Villa Belvedere with Carlo and his family was to be a visit to Herculaneum and Pompeii and so once again we headed down the hill to the station at Sant'Agnello to catch the train north along the Bay of Naples.

We knew the routine: first we stopped off at the tobacconist's to buy our scratch-card parking tickets for the whole day then on to where we'd parked the last time we'd done this trip, just round the corner from the station. Except that this time it was market day and all the parking spaces were underneath the stalls. So we drove on a bit, round a few corners, down a few streets and all the time keeping a mental picture of our location in relation to the station; eventually we found a space, parked up, marked the scratch-cards, left them visible in the window, and made our way up and round to the station just as a train was pulling out.

We knew the trains were every half hour, plenty of time to get our tickets and go to the loo until, that is, we found ourselves in the queue behind the English-family-from-hell. First of all they weren't sure where they were going and then they didn't seem to know how many there were in their group and whether or not they were adults or children and then all

Herculaneum and Pompeii, almost as they were two thousand years ago

those foreign coins and notes were such a bother ... and of course they expected that the man in the ticket office should be both patient *and* communicate with them in fluent English.

The next train came and went ... the family of indeterminate size and faculties were in fact going just one station in the opposite direction, to the terminus at Sorrento, and could have walked there in less time than they took to get their tickets. Another half-hour later and we were finally under way and heading for the Bay of Naples.

Before we left England a friend had told us that, to get a flavour of the devastation caused by the eruption of Vesuvius in 79CE, Herculanium was the site to visit rather than Pompeii. Not true.

What is true is that, if time is of the essence, the ruins of Herculanium are part of a smaller, more manageable site but otherwise there is no real comparison with Pompeii. We had allowed ourselves a morning in Herculanium – which, thanks to our various setbacks at Sant'Agnello, turned out to be an hour less than we had planned – and an afternoon at Pompeii; an afternoon was simply not enough.

That said, we did our best. We tried to be economical with the available time and squeezed in as much as possible in the certain knowledge that we would never see it all. What we did manage to see left us in awe at the scale of the disaster that hit this city – it is estimated that the port of Pompeii had around 20,000 inhabitants at the time of the eruption.

But it is the clarity with which the mind's eye is able to reconstruct this place that takes you by surprise; here there is no need for computer graphics to appreciate the size and scale of the important structures such as the Forum, the Temple of Jupiter and the Villa of the Mysteries; no need for a map to experience the broad thoroughfares, the side streets, the shops and the alleyways; no need for a guidebook to wonder at the beauty and diversity of the countless murals and mosaics. All you need is time and imagination and then, when you happen upon the plaster casts of the carbonised bodies that were unearthed at the time of the original excavations, all you need is compassion for the people who lived, loved and died here almost two thousand years ago.

As our train headed back to Sant'Agnello, my mind was still wrestling with images of Pompeii, not just as we'd seen it that day but also as the setting for Robert Harris' remarkable novel, *Pompeii*, which I was reading at the time. Set just before and during the eruption, Harris paints a picture of a city oblivious to its fate, a city used to rumblings from nearby Vesuvius, a prosperous city, a vibrant port focused on the present rather than what was just around the corner. Sometimes fiction paints the best picture.

I also had fleeting visions of another Pompeii, the Pompeii of the comedian Frankie Howerd and his irreverent creation, the slave Lurcio. For half an hour every week in the early 1970s, the nation it seemed came to a standstill as colourful tongue-in-cheek characters, masters and mistresses of the *double entendre*, sent up the city of Pompeii. I had seen signs and sites around Pompeii that afternoon that triggered memories of the fictional *Up Pompeii!* and wondered whether its creator, Talbot Rothwell, had done a lot more research than may have been supposed. Who knows.

We arrived back at Sant'Agnello and retraced our steps to the car, a ten-minute walk from the station.

Kay saw it first – they just look the same in all languages – a parking ticket tucked neatly behind a windscreen wiper. Sitting in the car we read the indictment, that we'd been parked there all day without a permit and now had to pay a fine of €20.

In case I'd inadvertently scratched off the wrong date or

times, I scrutinised every box of the scratch-card permits we'd bought earlier but everything seemed fine. Then, out of the corner of my eye in the car's wing-mirror, I saw the parking attendant heading our way. Politely and with a touch of 'we're just simple-minded foreigners, guv' we confronted him with the evidence: our parking permits correctly completed and his parking ticket implying the opposite.

He looked at both and nodded, he could see that we'd completed them correctly and said as much but, he went on to explain, the permits we had used were for the *comune* of Sant'Agnello and we were now parked up in the adjacent *comune* of Piano di Sorrento which had, of course, its own customised permits. By having to drive a little bit further to find a parking space earlier in the day, *after* we'd bought the scratch-cards, we had innocently crossed an undefined border into a different *comune*.

He was a sympathetic young man, *un ragazzo simpatico,* and could appreciate how we'd come to make such a mistake but, having issued the ticket, there was nothing he could do – we'd have to pay the fine. I took out my wallet ... but, no, we couldn't pay him, we'd have to go the municipal offices to do that and so he wrote down the address and gave us directions round the one-way system. He also suggested that we might try to argue our case there.

On the third lap of Piano di Sorrento we found it, except that there was nowhere to park. I was rapidly losing the will to live so did what any Italian driver would have done in such circumstances: I parked up anyway and left Kay in the car to explain things should another parking attendant turn up.

I went into the office and managed to collar a genial-looking, bearded fifty-something who listened to my story and, like his colleague, he understood how such a thing could have happened and, clearly a lateral thinker, he was of the opinion that it was unfair and that we should not have to pay any fine at all. Confident that he could sort it, he gathered together all the paperwork and strode into a back office where his superior was lording it over an empty desk and a phone. I could see him trying to explain the situation and the shrug-of-the-shoulders response that his boss gave which clearly meant, '... and what do you want me to do about it?'. More animated and audible discussions ensued and I could feel there was definitely 'previous' between these two and I knew who was going to win.

My hero returned to the front counter, shrugged his shoulders and apologised ... he'd done his best but I'd have to pay the fine. As I took my credit card out of my wallet, he shook his head and waved his finger – cash only. I didn't have the cash, nor did Kay, so I asked him where the nearest bank was and hoofed it about a half a kilometre down the road, quickly explaining to Kay where I was going as I passed the car.

When I returned and finally paid the fine, my hero was nowhere to be seen so I crossed behind the counter (nobody seemed to notice or mind) and wandered up and down corridors, poking my head round every door until I found him. I went over and shook his hand and thanked him once again for doing his best; he shrugged his shoulders for the umpteenth time that day and said, "*La vita è così*". Yes, life *is* like that.

The day still not done, it was two weary travellers who eventually unlocked the gate into the courtyard at Villa Belvedere; the household pet, a bouncy dalmation, opened a solitary disinterested eye in recognition. Inside the apartment we slumped into armchairs, separately mulling over a day to remember, unaware that worse was to come. I took out my camera and began to flick through images of Herculanium and then Pompeii ... I decided to delete one and instead deleted them all. In vain I sought the 'undo' button but this was a camera, not a computer.

This day was going from bad to worse. Crestfallen I took a shower.

It was gone eight when we left the apartment, descended the marble steps and crossed the courtyard towards the security gate; the dog was still dozing. I was a little ahead of Kay so that I could press the button that, from the inside only, automatically released the lock on the gate. We think it was the audible click of the gate that triggered what happened next.

Kay, being that little bit closer, heard it just before I did. It was the unmistakeable pounding of paws, fast and aggressive. Next moment the hitherto placid and user-friendly family pet was barking excitedly while sinking his paws and claws into Kay's back. Pandemonium broke loose as the dog ran off and I helped a very shaken Kay to her feet while at the same time Carlo rushed out to help while his father retrieved the dog and tied it to a tree.

Kay's top was ripped and there was clearly blood underneath. Amid all the apologies and offers of help, I explained that we had antiseptic and plasters with us and ushered Kay back to our apartment to assess the damage. It was not as bad as we feared but bad enough; there was substantial bruising and the skin was broken and bleeding, all of which our holiday first-aid kit coped with. With Kay bandaged and both recovered we decided to try that once again; we needed to eat almost as much as we needed a large glass of red wine.

The dog remained tied up and Carlo and his father were still there waiting for us as, once again, we headed for the gate. They were clearly upset and genuinely perplexed about the whole incident; they were sure that the dog had never done this before and, anyway, he knew us, we'd been in and out many times. I tried to explain that I thought it was the sudden noise of the gate being unlocked that had broken his sleep – it had just come at the wrong moment and he had probably reacted instinctively.

A quarter of an hour later we were down in the town, the red wine on the table; we were just about to start our second glass.

It was gone eleven when we were returned to Villa Belvedere. We unlocked the gate a little more carefully and slowly than usual; all seemed quiet ... until, that is, we started to cross the courtyard. Out of the apartment below ours came Carlo, his father and his mother, *la mamma,* still adjusting a hastily thrown on dressing gown; they had clearly been waiting for us.

The apologies continued but they wanted us to talk to Carlo's sister on *il telefonino* ... we'd met Roseanna once before and knew that they were right, her English *was* better. She explained that the dog was 'clean', in other words he had had all the right jabs and at the right time but that, just in case, Kay should have a tetanus injection. Kay explained that it was her intention to go straight to her doctor when we returned home in two days time. But Roseanna was insistent, it was important to have the tetanus injection now, certainly within twenty-four hours.

She was right, of course, and went on to explain that they would pay for the sterilised anti-tetanus 'kit' from the pharmacy and that *la mamma* would administer the injection the following morning. Her mother nodded profusely and smiled a knowing smile ... it's never quite what you expect.

Our initial negative reaction towards this suggestion was soon dispelled when Roseanna explained that her mother did all the injections in the family and always had *and* that she was very, very good, better than any doctor. It was this last bit that persuaded Kay and so an appointment was made for ten in the morning when the needle-wielding *mamma* would appear.

La mamma arrived bang on schedule. In the light of day and sporting her normal day attire, she looked infinitely more the part than she had in her pastel-pink dressing gown the night before.

First of all she showed us that the packet had not been opened and that its contents were therefore sterile. She washed her hands and forcefully ushered me out of the apartment while Kay stood nervously awaiting her fate.

Outside I chatted to Carlo, clearly still perturbed by these strange and embarrassing events and perhaps worried too that we might have some future litigation in mind. I also kept an ear to the apartment door half expecting to hear a scream at any moment. None came.

A few moments later a beaming *mamma* appeared, the deed done. Behind her back Kay gave me a thumbs-up sign ... and later explained that it was the most painless injection she'd ever had.*

An hour later, clutching our ten perdent discount voucher for any future stay at Villa Belvedere, we were once again heading north towards Rome and Ciampino Airport ... I had an appointment the next morning with the dentist.

---

*In southern Italy such an arrangement is quite common: where one family member, usually *la mamma* or *la nonna* (grandmother), would become adept at giving the injections and, provided the treatment was routine, as it was in our case, then everybody would become used to having their jabs at home rather than in the doctor's surgery. People suffering from diabetes often have their daily insulin jabs administered by a family member or neighbour.

A quiet corner of Otranto and a quiet cove nearby

Otranto

We kept our appointment in September with Gino with a week back in Corigliano d'Otranto though this time we had to spend three nights in one of his town apartments before returning to our favourite little retreat in the countryside. Gino had clearly overbooked and unfortunately for us his other guests got there first.

We were still in touch with Francesca from the UK but decided not to mention this short trip; once again we just wanted a break from work and to enjoy the late summer Italian sun. We realised there was a chance we might bump into each other but thought this unlikely given her apparent lack of affection for Corigliano.

Apart from moving mid-stay, we completed our visits to the other Greek towns in the Salento and enjoyed eating every night in the *same* restaurant ... yes, finally we had agreed on the best place to eat in Corigliano. It was here on our first meal, post-agreement, that we got talking to Marco and his 14-year old daughter Gabriella. It was almost obligatory to strike up some sort of conversation for, on the mezzanine floor, we were the only four people.

Marco hailed from Otranto where he was a judge and

Gabriella and her younger sister (who wasn't there that evening) appeared to live in both Otranto and Gallipoli where their mother worked. We never quite got to the bottom of the domestic situation; it could have been a separation or simply a work or schooling arrangement but, whichever, it seemed to suit everybody. We talked mainly about Corigliano and Otranto: for us Corigliano was the place we like to stay and Otranto on the east coast the place we most liked to visit; for Marco it was the exact opposite – he lived in Otranto and liked to come to Corigliano of an evening to eat, particularly at this restaurant which he reckoned served the best food in this part of the Salento.

Both Marco and Gabriella spoke good English so our conversation was less riddled with infinitives and wild guesses. Marco was particularly intrigued about how it was that we discovered Corigliano d'Otranto in the first place. He explained that it was a little oasis hereabouts that had something 'different' but, like us, he couldn't pinpoint that difference, it was just a feeling that we shared.

We went on to talk about the delights of Otranto and Marco suggested that we visit him there that Saturday and that, weather-permitting, we could go out on his boat and get a different perspective of the eastern coast. Before we went our separate ways we exchanged telephone numbers and Marco said that he'd call on the Friday to finalise arrangements.

As we walked back to our apartment we talked about the evening and first of all tried to make a stab at guessing Marco's age. He seemed to be in his mid-forties but did they have judges that young in Italy? We didn't know. Then we speculated about whether or not he actually would get in touch again for the thought of sitting back, glass in hand, on the iridescent Mare Adriatico was appealing ... perhaps less so to Kay who is not such a good sailor. Also it crossed our minds that somehow, yet again, we had been taken on board (seemingly literally in this case) by a complete stranger. It was beginning to seem like some sort of affliction.

As arranged, Marco called on the Friday and we agreed to meet by the castle in Otranto at ten the next morning.

Saturday dawned. It was a beautiful summery day, scarcely a breeze, the temperature beginning its climb up into the low thirties ... we headed to Otranto, parked up and got to the castle right on time. When, by ten past ten, there was no sign of Marco we began to wonder whether we were in the right place for there were seemingly two entrances to the castle. Experience had taught us that Italian meeting arrangements have a unique fluidity both in terms of time and place and, to coin a phrase, are rarely what you expect ... so Kay stayed where we thought we should be and I began flitting between her the other possible meeting point, all the time trying to recall exactly what Marco looked like.

On my third lap, heading back towards Kay around ten-thirty, I spotted him ambling along the footpath heading our way. Greetings over he explained that we would go back to his apartment to get the food ready and meet up with some other people who were also going out on the boat. This boat was getting bigger and bigger all the time.

At Marco's apartment we met his other daughter and a couple of her friends as well as another, slightly older, slightly greyer, but equally amiable, judge and Marco's housekeeper who was busy preparing a sort of late breakfast for everyone (including us) as well as getting together some baskets of goodies for lunch at sea. It was gone half eleven when our little group (minus the housekeeper) finally headed for the harbour.

As we approached the quayside Kay and I both had painted mental pictures of Marco's boat and were looking forward to sitting up on deck in the sun watching the world go by; we knew we were fortunate to be here at all with this generous group of people. Everyone stopped for a break by a small row of rubber dinghies tied to the stone jetty ... at least *we* assumed it was a break for all the larger craft were a bit further on and some were anchored a short distance mid-harbour. But no, Marco's boat was indeed this very rubber dinghy complete with a massive outboard motor and I then I realised that we must be going out on the dinghy to a larger boat anchored in the harbour ... I just wasn't sure which one.

With everyone aboard we headed off, weaving slowly around other boats and all the time heading for the harbour entrance; the girls were already in sunbathing mode but it wasn't until we passed the end of the harbour pier that the penny finally dropped ... this *was* Marco's boat. And Marco was a boy racer at heart. Seconds after crossing the imaginary line that was the entrance to the harbour, Marco put his foot on the gas, the outboard responded noisily, the bow of the boat shot up into the air and we were off.

This was not what either of us had pictured when we woke up that morning; everyone else seemed to be loving it but Kay, at sea not her location of choice, was hanging on for grim death as was I, a better sailor but a non-swimmer.

At breakneck speed we headed along the coast north from Otranto, surging past lesser craft who clearly didn't have a madman as a skipper. After about fifteen terrifying minutes skimming across the Mare Adriatico we stopped for a few blissful moments alongside a much larger craft, the sort of boat we *thought* we were going out on, while Marco did a bit of socialising with his friends. As we pulled away Marco explained that he'd arranged that we'd stop off here for an *aperitivo* later in the afternoon on our way back to Otranto. Kay and I couldn't wait ... we weren't sure we'd last that long without a drink!

Like a bat out of hell, Marco was off again but after five minutes he slowed up as we approached an exquisite, secluded sandy cove, its offshore peppered with small boats like ours, most of their occupants already in the sea or lying on the small arc of golden sand. We dropped anchor a hundred metres offshore.

Within seconds everyone aboard Marco's boat was ready to take the plunge; everybody, that is, except Kay and I. We had been expecting a sightseeing trip, it had simply never occurred to us that this outing was basically an opportunity to sunbathe and cool off in the water. As a non-swimmer, the urge to jump in the sea was not something that came naturally and Kay, who does swim, hadn't thought to bring her costume – it was safely tucked up in a drawer in England.

As (bad) luck would have it, Enzo, the other judge, came to my rescue when he announced that he was pretty sure he had brought two costumes and proceeded to rummage away in the depths of his bag, then let out a whoop of delight as he proudly waved aloft his spare pair *and* he had a spare towel too! He knew I would be overcome with gratitude and would have none of my futile protestations ... it was nothing, *di niente*, what are friends for? There was no escape, I'd have to show my appreciation for this act of kindness and plunge my pristine-white body into the Mare Adriatico.

As I slipped into Enzo's trunks everyone was already in the water doing their own thing: the girls had met up with some friends from other boats; Marco had already made it ashore and was chatting up a young female friend and Enzo was circling the boat waiting for someone to play with ... me. I asked Enzo how deep it was so he stood up to show me that the water came up to his neck ... I reckoned I was slightly shorter than Enzo but that I would probably get away with it. Plunge I did not. Ever so slowly, a fake grin on my face disguising the fear in my eyes, I slipped over the side, one hand firmly holding on to the boat until I found the soft sandy bottom with the tips of my toes.

I walked ashore.

Truth be told, I had a great time in the water that day and really wished I could do more than walk and make futile, half-hearted attempts at getting my feet off the bottom for any length of time. Kay was the one that missed out and although she enjoyed sitting in the boat, the sun to herself, she made a mental note to pack her costume next time.

It was soon time to eat and dry off back on the boat; simple fare it was – bread, cheese, ham, tomatoes, water and wine – exactly what we all needed. For the adults, an extra glass of wine was what was called for; for the girls a last plunge into the sea to say goodbye to their friends, and then, the anchor safely on board, we headed back, at a more sedate pace this time, to the boat we'd stopped at earlier.

This was a proper boat with tables and chairs and cabins and a fridge, a toilet and an engine hidden out of sight somewhere – the sort of boat Kay and I had thought that Marco was sure to have. Once again we sat in the late afternoon sun, shared a few nibbles, a few stories, a few glasses until, that is, the girls got restless and threatened mutiny unless we headed back home. The 'big' boat finally evacuated, Kay and I clung on for dear life as Marco opened up the throttle for the big finale as once again we shot across the water like a bullet from a gun, the entrance to Otranto's harbour our fast-approaching respite.

Back on terra firma, Marco invited us to have a pizza with him that evening in Otranto but we had to decline as we had arranged with Gino that we'd move into the *villette* in the countryside when we got back.

As we returned to Corigliano we wished we could have

stayed in Otranto with Marco and Enzo and the girls; yes, we were looking forward to being back in the countryside but could have done without having to load up the car and unpack it again.

Still, it was a day that, for all sorts of reasons, we would never forget. It was a day that, once again, was not what we were expecting but in a funny sort of way it was a typically Italian day. The Italians love to play and they love to share the things that give them the greatest pleasure and a brief encounter with two complete strangers in a restaurant is enough to trigger this openness and generosity. The fact that we got it all wrong and hadn't anticipated a bare-knuckle ride with a genial madman at the helm was our problem and one that we, as non-Italians, would always have to cope with.

We had a lot to learn about these people and this place; and it was people like Marco, Gino and Salvatore at Sciacca, people open enough to share some of what it meant to them, who were our generous teachers.

Our final three days at our favourite little hideaway in the countryside were exactly what we wanted and needed – lots of sun and lots of doing nothing other than trips in and out of the town and the odd encounter with people we knew like Nicola, Isabella and Mareka.

When, once again, the time came to say goodbye to Gino that tear returned to his eye ... maybe it was because he didn't want us to go; maybe it was because, for the first time, he didn't have the dates of our next visit in his pocket.

TUSCANY

UMBRIA

LAZIO

Rome

FRASCATI

Ciampino ● ○ ● Tuscolo
Grottaferrata

● *Lake Albano*
● *Lake Nemi*

*Tyrrhenian
Sea*

Anzio ●

Frascati to Anzio · 45km

A change of direction

As the end of the year approached we were both suffering from withdrawal symptoms and longed to get back to Italy just for a few days. The most southerly destination from Bristol was Rome Ciampino with easyJet but then the long drive south always ate into our time by at least two days so we decided that we'd look for somewhere to stay just south of Rome that might offer us something different. That 'somewhere' was Frascati.

Apart from odd nights close to airports, we'd never actually stayed for any length of time in a hotel so we chose to break another habit and booked into the Hotel Flora, less than half an hour's drive from the airport.

Frascati sits atop a broad hill overlooking Rome and is part of the area know as the Castelli Romani (Castles of Rome); it is also known for its DOC-status* white wines of the same name. That is about as much as we knew when, on a cool brisk evening in early February, we stepped into the elegant Hotel Flora to be welcomed by a bubbly receptionist

---

*DOC – *Denominazione di origine controllata*, controlled origin denomination – is the Italian equivalent of the French AOC (*Appellation d'origine contrôlée*) and guarantees a level of quality that requires that the wine be produced to specific standards, normally within a particular region and using defined methods.

from south Wales. We were eager to get out into the town and eat so, Kay's Welsh connections dispensed with and after we'd thrown our bags in our room, Glenys pointed us in the direction of Il Pinocchio in the Piazza del Mercato where we ate that first night and every night thereafter.

Not surprisingly, the restaurant paid homage to a certain little long-nosed pre-Disney puppet; from floor to ceiling the place bulged with images and models (including a human-sized statuette) of the colourful precocious little brat*. Normally one meal in such a place would have been enough for us but here the food was both excellent and reasonably priced ... and then there was Gaetano.

Gaetano was one of three brothers who ran Il Pinocchio, except that he 'ran' it from his state-of-the-art wheelchair that he controlled from a little joystick on its arm. Like Marco in Otranto and Schumacher in Germany, Gaetano had a penchant for speed and he put this to good use as he raced between and round tables and backwards and forwards from the door to greet his guests.

With panache, precision timing and eyes and ears that missed nothing, he organised the waiters, chatted to his regulars and kept tabs on the kitchen. When things were quiet he shot down to the back of the restaurant to keep his spirited mother company and performed a remarkable handbrake turn as he deftly snuggled up against the old-fashioned wooden desk and till that she manned ... in all probability the same desk that was *in situ* to collect the cash when the restaurant opened in 1935.

After our second visit Gaetano elevated us to 'regular'

---

*When Carlo Collodi wrote *Pinocchio* in the 1880s it was essentially a pedagogic work with overtly political overtones, one of many written in the wake of Italian reunification (1860) with the aim of galvanising Italian patriotism through notions of hard work and self-sacrifice.

status and spent much of his time chatting to us; he also introduced me to his grappa menu and insisted that I work my way through it. Who was I to argue?

That first evening we decided to take a late stroll through some of Frascati's back streets, looking for somewhere warm to have a nightcap. We heard music and eventually found its source, a small bar in a side-street that was either open or closed, it was difficult to tell which. With our noses stuck to door-window we could see a small group of people sitting or standing round a couple of tables, some were strumming guitars, others were singing, there were glasses of red wine on the table ... all the hallmarks of a private and impromptu jam session or the dying embers of a birthday bash. We were just about to move on when the door opened and we tumbled in, without hesitation accepting the invitation to stay and have a drink or three.

Neither of us remember much more after that: we recall the fact that being from the UK was some sort of bonus; we recall being asked to sing something English and becoming mute at the very thought; we recall some eccentric individuals and in particular one short, ageing and overweight rocker who arrived late with his guitar (which he never played) and was convinced that we might have the contacts to find him a few gigs in the UK; we recall the flattering pre-paunch painting of the bar's owner on the wall; we recall that our glasses were never empty for very long; and finally we just about recall returning to the hotel in the wee small hours, not all that long after we stepped off the plane, and thinking that already we were in need of a holiday!

The Castelli Romani are a group of sixteen *comune* that sit on the broad fertile hills (the Colli Albani) south and east of Rome. The area was once volcanic and the two lakes in the

Walking the walk in Frascati

region, Albano and the smaller Nemi, are in fact water-filled craters.

We visited both lakes and took a walk by Albano, overseen by the Pope's summer residence at Castel Gandolfo, before lunching overlooking the sinister-looking Nemi where both Julius Caesar and Caligula took a little time off from the conspiratorial niceties of Rome. Two of Caligula's massive pleasure barges were found at the bottom of Nemi and during the Mussolini era were salvaged and housed at a specially built museum until they were destroyed by fire towards the end of the second World War.

We visited too the coastal town of Anzio which also has a wartime history as the site of the allied landings which eventually, and following heavy losses on both sides, led to the march north to Rome and, coincidentally, the loss of the Nemi ships. One side of the ensuing argument suggests that their destruction was a deliberate act by retreating German troops, the other that advancing American artillery was the culprit. I blame the excessive Caligula for having such extravagant tastes and building them in the first place.

Early evening and its time for the people of Frascati to partake of the *passeggiata*, to dress up and head towards the open spaces around Piazza Roma and Piazza Guglielmo Marconi to promenade and gossip with style and more than a mere hint of theatre and, as ever, with an eye to who's out and who's in, who's talking to whom and, ears sharp as radar, who or what they're talking about.

Although we had experienced the *passeggiata* before, it was here in Frascati where it seemed to have become almost an artform. Two things were different, the time of year and the number of women on parade; and these two were not unconnected. It being February it was cold and for many of Frascati's womenfolk of a certain age this was an opportunity to show off their fur. And show it off they most certainly did.

Usually in pairs, and with a panache that lacked any hint of embarrassment or concession to being (or not being) politically correct, they strolled gracefully up and down. Many of these fur-framed ladies trailed furry little pooches on leads which in turn, bearing in mind the season, needed to be decked out in the right gear ... nothing as indiscreet as fur on fur of course, that would be a little over the top, but tartan seemed to be both 'in' and appropriate.

Still further behind were the menfolk. They knew their place and kept their distance in the certain knowledge that this was not their show. But they had a function, their job was to carry the umbrella and be ready, at the merest hint of rain, to protect their good lady (and their investment) from the elements.

Although it was the fur-clad womenfolk that caught our eye, many other *frascatani* were out and about: young and old, families with children, work colleagues, smouldering couples, doting grandparents, all chatting, wheeling and dealing, gesticulating extravagantly, renewing friendships, making calls, exchanging glances.

Wherever you see it, the *passeggiata* has a rhythm that is dictated not just by the people, the season and the local culture but also by the space within and around which people are walking. There is a place to turn, an undefined, invisible mini-roundabout where people stop, turn and begin the process all over again; there is a subtle order to this apparently haphazard flow of humanity that somehow avoids collisions and last-minute changes of direction. It is a daily ritual that has no beginning, no end and involves no planning. It is uniquely Italian and, for the outsider, singularly compulsive viewing ... and, should you decide to join in, there is no impediment and no charge.

Despite my attempt to set fire to the place, Il Pinocchio continued to be our restaurant of choice. On our third evening there, I was leaning across the table to chat to Gaetano, momentarily parked up alongside Kay opposite, and with my attention thus focused across and down, I failed to notice that the menu I had been perusing was now dancing alongside the flame of the candle. A scream from an adjacent table alerted us to the fact that the menu was now on fire and of course, to make matters worse, I then dropped the fireball onto the tablecloth while, quick as a flash, Gaetano swung round his chariot to snatch a glass of water from another table with which to finally put an end to these embarrassing events.

Embarrassment competed with half-hearted laughter and profuse apologies as things got back to normal and a bemused waitress changed our charred tablecloth. Gaetano, on the other hand, seemed not to mind and, having finally taken our order, returned to finish our conversation in which he had a pecuniary interest.

Il Pinocchio, it seemed, was more than a restaurant and offered basic accommodation and Gaetano wanted us to take a look in case we were ever back this way. What he didn't know was that Bristol to Rome Ciampino was the best route for us, even for the south of Italy, and that somewhere to stay close to the airport was the perfect overnight stop in both directions.

For obvious reasons Gaetano himself was unable to show us the rooms above the restaurant so we arranged to come back the next day around lunchtime when one of his brothers would do the honours. The rooms were clean, had all the essentials but were not over-endowed with sunlight (no bad thing at the height of the summer) but, as a stopover or a base from which to explore Frascati and the Castelli Romani, they were ideal and I was already mentally planning our next trip down to Apulia.

Driving in and around Frascati it was impossible not to notice the frequency of the word 'Tuscolana' (or a variant) on roadside signage, indeed our hotel was on Via Tuscolana. Also, on my atlas, a small archaeological site was marked with the name 'Tuscolo'. We were curious and were therefore always on the lookout for one of those brown signs that, in Italy, always point to something of historical interest.

When we eventually happened upon the 'Tuscolo' sign it was a bonus but experience had taught us that finding the first sign was only the beginning of the little game that the installers of such signage like to have with visitors, be they Italian or otherwise. Over the years I have developed a theory as to how this particularly Italian phenomenon works, or rather why it doesn't work as you might reasonably expect it to.

Let us say they are six turnings from the main road to a particular site and that each turning warrants a directional sign. Unfortunately whoever counts the turnings forgets about the one off the main road and only orders five signs. Of course the one off the main road is the most important so when the signs are fixed in place, one of the other turnings has to remain sign-less. That's my theory anyway ... on the other hand there could just be someone coursing the countryside collecting one sign for every historical site.

In search of Tuscolo we encountered, not for the first time, the scourge of the missing sign, a point between main road and destination where you have to guess the next move. So our route up to Tuscolo involved a couple of three-point turns, a bit of back-tracking here and there and a modicum of guesswork but, in the end, we found it.

Once an important satellite of Rome and with a history

dating back to the 8th and 7th centuries BCE, Tusculum was the original home to many of the city's noble families, including Cato the Elder and Cicero. Today the ruins are centred around a small ampitheatre, all that indiscriminate invaders, mediæval recyclers and the onward march of nature and erratic climate changes have left behind. Nevertheless it is an impressive hilltop site, in part because of the stillness and the peace, in part because of the spectacular views of the Roman countryside. It was these rather than the ruins themselves that brought us back to this tranquil hilltop later in the year.

We sought out the 'musical' bar one more time but it was like stepping into an altogether different world, a quiet, sparsely populated world ... just like any other bar that night in Frascati. Gone was the music, the bonhomie, the raised voices and the laughter; we recognised no-one, nobody recognised us. It was as if that first night, that special occasion that we had somehow stumbled upon had never happened ... the only reassurance that we were in the same place was the portrait of the owner on the wall and the fact that the wine was *sfuso*, served directly from a barrel.

Our last night came and went. We ate at Il Pinocchio, I sampled another *grappa* or three and Gaetano made sure we left with some of his business cards should we ever decide to return this way.

We had a late afternoon flight back to Bristol so planned to revisit the small town of Grottaferrata, which we liked a lot and to which we had gravitated several times, before heading to Lake Albano for lunch and another lakeside walk in the warm spring-like sunshine. From Albano it was no more than a fifteen-minute drive down to today's incarnation of the Via Appia and on to Ciampino Airport.

As we were driving to the airport I realised we'd been on this road once before, or rather the other end of this road, for the original Via Appia linked Rome and Brindisi in Apulia where a couple of years earlier we'd stood by the pillar marking its end on the Mare Adriatico.

Via Appia, strategically one of the most important of the early Roman roads, was started in 312 BCE and reached Brindisi in 264 BCE and it was along this northern stretch, between Rome and Capua, that the ex-gladiator Spartacus and some 6000 of his followers were crucified in 71 BCE.

I saw the film *Spartacus* several times in the 60s but nothing compares with the novel of the same name by Howard Fast on which it was based. Fast, a black-listed American writer in the McCarthy era who had to self-publish the book, tells the story through the eyes of four noted Roman aristocrats including the aforementioned Cicero from Tusculum.

As we sat preparing for take-off in the shadow of the Alban Hills, dissected by so many incarnations of the Via Appia, my thoughts were elsewhere. I made a mental note to find a copy of *Spartacus* and then to read again all the other novels by Fast that were so important to me at that time.

Somewhere over the Bay of Biscay we decided that in the summer we should try something new; much as we liked it, we'd give the Salento a break and, with our brief sojourn in Frascati as a beacon, find fresh pastures.

From heel to toe

The decision not to go to the Salento was the easy part, exactly where to go proved more difficult. We still wanted to travel south so the three options seemed to be, another part of Apulia, (perhaps the Gargano peninsula in the north), Basilicata or Calabria. Or we could, of course, return to Sicily.

We eventually opted for Calabria and, to reduce the driving time from Rome, were thinking initially of the north-western part of the region*. This all changed when we realised that, if we were to base ourselves further south, we could kill two birds with one stone and go across to Sicily for a few days to finally experience an open-air Greek tragedy at Siracusa's stunning Teatro Greco.

We were also considering booking half-board (bed, breakfast and evening meal) at an *agriturismo* rather than renting an apartment or *villetta* and eating out every evening. Over the years we had become accustomed to seeing the signs for *agriturismi* (and *masserie* as they are often called in Apulia) and had even eaten in one with Francesca and Ciccio.

---

*Apulia, Basilicata and Calabria are, like Toscana, called *regioni* (regions) in Italy and *regioni* are made up of *province* (provinces). Calabria, for example, has five *province*: Cosenza, Crotone, Catanzaro, Vibo Valentia and Reggio Calabria.

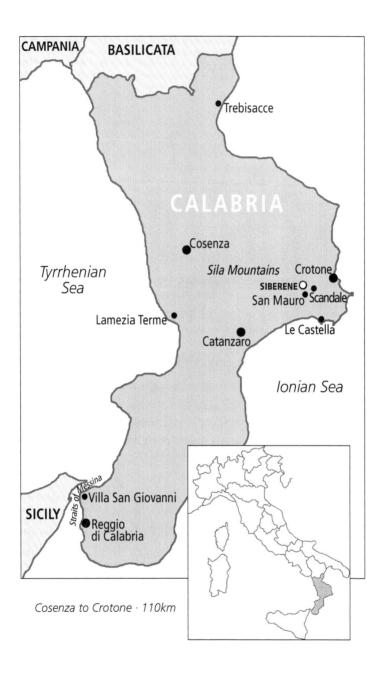

CAMPANIA

BASILICATA

Trebisacce

CALABRIA

Cosenza

Sila Mountains   Crotone

SIBERENE ○

San Mauro · Scandale

Tyrrhenian
Sea

Lamezia Terme

Catanzaro

Le Castella

Ionian Sea

Villa San Giovanni

SICILY

Reggio
di Calabria

Cosenza to Crotone · 110km

Perhaps we were getting lazy because the thought of dining in each evening and not having to drive anywhere to eat or decide on this or that restaurant was quite appealing.

And so it was, with these different options wandering round our heads, that Kay hit upon an *agriturismo*, name of L'Oenotri, close to the small hilltop town of Siberene, in the Calabrian province of Crotone. A few emails later and everything was set for our first Calabrian adventure.

Once again we would fly to Rome Ciampino, pick up a car and drive to Frascati for a night at Il Pinocchio; the following day we would drive south to Siberene where we would stay four days before continuing on south and across to Sicily for four nights before returning to Calabria and Siberene for eleven more days; finally, we would head back to Frascati for another two nights at Il Pinocchio before flying back to Bristol. I had also booked seats for a performance of Euripode's *Ecuba* on our last night in Siracusa. Or so I thought.

Of course we had been to Calabria before but at the time were in passing-through mode. En route to Sicily we had flown to Lamezia Terme a couple of times and stayed overnight at the hotel opposite the station before driving down to either Reggio di Calabria or Villa San Giovanni to catch the ferry to Messina. I don't think it ever occurred to either of us that we were passing through a separate region of Italy. Traversing the western seaboard of Calabria had been a means to an end rather than an end in itself.

And so it was that when we finally crossed into Calabria on the *autostrada* we were viewing things with a new eye, not least because much of the road itself seemed to be in the grip of never-ending roadworks.

We left the *autostrada* north of Cosenza and, on the second attempt, having finally disentangled ourselves from the city's complex and erratically-signed road network, headed out east to cross the breathtaking Sila mountains.

To describe the Sila as 'breathtaking' barely does it justice. Add to the landscape the strength and simplicity of the high-stilted *superstrada* that dares to take you up and through these majestic wooded peaks and across deep, primordial valleys, verdant and solitary, and it does almost take your breath away. Road and landscape complement each other ... we could not have experienced one without the other.

We passed a sign saying we had reached the road's highest point, 1427 metres above sea level, before starting the descent towards Crotone and soon afterwards left the *superstrada* to cut across country on a narrow, serpentine road, the last lap to Siberene.

As we drove past the turning up to Siberene itself and the sign indicating we were a mere kilometre away from L'Oenotri, we were still in awe of the views of the town that came and went the closer we got. And then there was that one final panorama of the massive, uncompromising slab of rock, the town clinging on hopefully to its summit, its buildings illuminated by the golden-pink, late afternoon sun.

Still in shock, we pulled off the road and into L'Oenotri's car park where we were greeted by a large alsatian and a ruddy-faced man, late-thirties, with a bandaged hand.

Roberto made sure the dog, Mara, kept her distance as he sought out the diminutive, elegant co-owner, Beniamina, who showed us to our room overlooking a small garden no more than ten metres from the pool. Before we unpacked I asked Kay if she was happy to remain here, bearing in mind her recent experience with the dog at Sant'Agata. I confess that I was none too happy myself for I have never found it easy to be around dogs, particularly large dogs, since an unfortunate under-table incident when I was a youngster.

We decided to stay and spent the next couple of hours relaxing by the pool or wandering round the grounds, eyeing up the fruit trees, the vines and the chickens. It had been a hard six-hour drive from Frascati and all we wanted to do was eat, drink a few glasses of wine and go to bed. Beniamina introduced us her brother Vincenzo, who ran L'Oenotri on a day-to-day basis, and later to the chef, Salvatore, who told us that dinner would be served just after eight.

Vincenzo explained how Agriturismo l'Oenotri had once been a working farm that had fallen into decay and that he and his family renovated and modernised it and its outbuildings to create this little oasis on the outskirts of Siberene. The name l'Oenotri refers to an ancient Italian people who lived in this part of the peninsula and who inherited a countryside rich in vines.

In addition, this part of Calabria, and particularly Siberene, was strategically and historically important and as such was fought over by everyone from the Greeks to the Romans, the Byzantines, the Arabs, the Venetians and the Normans. Today, apart from its commanding position, it is a just another small, unassuming Italian hill-top town. Or so we thought.

As we took our seats in the restaurant, overseen by the upright, no-nonsense waiter, Martino, we were momentarily unprepared for what was to follow. There was no menu on the table, simply bread, red wine and water. Salvatore was going to feed us, he was going to take us on a culinary journey through the traditional Italian five-course meal ... *antipasti*, *primo piatto*, *secondo piatto*, *dolce* and *liquore*.

He turned out to be an extraordinarily gifted cook and each and every evening thereafter we ate not only good local fresh food but dinners that had been conceived and created with empathy and by a master of his craft

In the evenings we also met Gabriella who helped Salvatore in the kitchen and also looked after all L'Oenotri's laundry and ironing. Gabriella and her family had lived in Germany for many years and she was a fluent German speaker so, because at the time my German was infinitely better than my Italian, she and I always spoke in German.

On the second evening Beniamina came over to ask us something which we just couldn't understand; she tried again and still we couldn't get our heads round what it was she wanted to know. She raised a finger to signify that she had just thought of a way round this impasse, left us and returned carrying a large book; she had brought L'Oenotri's ledger of reservations to the table.

Beniamina opened the ledger and pointed at our booking and in particular the four-day gap and with her shoulders and her hands asked us why we would be away for four days and where were we going? When I explained that we wanted to spend four days in Sicily, in Siracusa, she apologised ... of course ... four days in Sicily ... it's obvious now.

Beniamina went on to indicate that our room was not booked for that period so if we wanted to leave our bags and some clothes there and just take what we needed for Sicily then they would look after things for us. I cannot recall how many times we said *molto gentile* that evening ... for it was a really kind offer and one that we did indeed take her up on.

For our first few days at L'Oenotri we did little other than wind down after a hard year and a hard drive. We sat by the pool and read or talked to Roberto, who looked after the animals and the land, or Angela, who cleaned the rooms. We also met Vincenzo's partner Elvira who worked in Cosenza during the week and spoke excellent English. Beniamina's husband Vittorio, a surgeon in Crotone, also put in an appearance.

Neither Kay nor I are beach people; we like to walk by the sea out of season, but lying on a crowded beach with sand working its way into every orifice is not for us. Most of the Italians, Germans, Dutch and French we encountered seemed to be of the opposite persuasion and so it was that L'Oenotri's other guests disappeared after breakfast, preferring the sand-in-every-orifice option to the pool, and left us in charge.

Nor have Kay and I ever opted for the sort of poolside holiday that is the stuff of glossy brochures and television adverts; when we chose to stay at L'Oenotri, the pool was never a consideration, particularly so for me, a non-swimmer. But here we had it to ourselves, usually until late afternoon; we had an ancient olive tree for shade, a couple of chairs and a table and 'our' pool to cool off in. It was heaven, the more so because the view across the tree-studded valley below the pool and up to the nearby Monte Fuscaldo was not only breathtakingly beautiful but it had a peace and serenity that defy description. Suffice to say, the memory of that view kept me going for a year.

As our fellow holidaymakers returned from their pilgrimage to the sea and headed for the pool to wash the sand away, we would start to get ready for our visit up to Siberene itself.

The first time we stepped into the square, an oval square with the castle dominating one end and the church the other, we were looking for a bar and a pre-prandial *aperitivo*. There were four bars in the square, two at the castle end, one in the middle and one near the church. We chose the castle end and stood in the middle trying to make a decision and, for no particular reason that I can recall, headed for a table outside the Rosa dei Venti where we met Carlo for the first time.

Mid-thirties, ever-smiling, slightly overweight, *simpatico*, genuine ... such was the Carlo that we got to know and love. Not that first day but, gradually, over the next three weeks we, the three of us, embarked upon a lasting and genuine friendship.

We had hoped that Carlo might have a television inside in case we ever wanted to follow England's inevitable route to disaster in the World Cup. He didn't, but he pointed us across the square to the bar opposite and told us that Pino had a television, we could watch there. I recall thinking how generous it was of him to be happy for us to take our custom elsewhere. Until, that is, he told us later that he and Pino were cousins.

Back at L'Oenotri we discovered that when we had made our original email reservation we had not been 'talking' to Vincenzo as we thought but to Elvira. This turned out to be a blessing in disguise for she was able to help me with a little problem regarding my Teatro Greco booking ... I realised I had mistakenly booked tickets for a date when we were actually still in Calabria and not Sicily. Somehow I had mixed up our 'last night' in Sicily with our 'last night' in Calabria.

So, using Elvira's computer, we were able to contact our hostess-to-be in Siracusa, explain the problem and hope that by the time we got there she might have been able to perform some sort of miracle and change the tickets for us.

Our routines were no sooner established, than it was time to pack up again and head for Sicily. We said our goodbyes as if we had already been there for a fortnight and trusted our room and our belongings to this unique little Calabrian family. We already knew that somehow we had found a very special place; just how special we would dicsover later.

We gave one last wave and headed into the gathering gloom. Within minutes the rain started. Calabrian rain.

To be or not to be

First we drove south and west towards and round Calabria's regional capital, Catanzaro, then on towards Lamezia to pick up the *autostrada* south towards the toe and the ferry to Sicily. And all the time the rain was getting heavier, pounding the car mercilessly.

The further south we got, the worse it got. Southern Italians do not generally like driving in the rain and so, between the roadworks, it was not unusual to see cars parked up on the hard shoulder, their drivers, mobile invariably to ear, elaborating on their plight to friends and family. We pressed on, ever hopeful that it might be different in Sicily as we planned to revisit Etna en route to Siracusa.

We could not even see Etna as we drove south down the east coast of Sicily and past where, on a clear day, we thought Etna should be. We arrived at our destination, the B&B Giuggiulena, earlier than expected and just as the rain was beginning to fall in a more civilised fashion. We parked up and never used the car again until we returned to Calabria.

My first concern was whether or not our hostess here, Sabrina, had been able to resolve the ticket situation at the Teatro Greco. She confirmed that she had managed to cancel our reservation in time but that as yet no replacement booking had materialised. She assured us that her friend who worked in the box office was on the case and was trying to find us seats for the performance on our last night in Sicily.

And, she explained, there was more good news: the next day the wind would change, overnight the scirocco from Africa would chase the rain away and within twenty-four hours everybody would be complaining about the heat instead.

Located at the end of a short cul-de-sac, from the outside B&B Giuggiulena looked like any other building in an area clearly trying to re-invent itself. It was a pleasant part of town, right on the sea and about three hundred metres from the bridge across to Ortigia, the ancient island settlement that we knew and loved.

Inside was a revelation – modern, clean, bright and intimate with wonderful sea-views from the spacious glass-fronted communal area and its balcony, the rooftop terrace and the bedrooms. Just along the road there was a water-taxi across to Ortigia, no more than five minutes away on a tranquil sea. Of course the taxi timetable had an erratic element or, to put it another way, was virtually non-existent, but it didn't matter for the bridge was only about ten minutes's walk away.

We were so pleased to be back here and spent the days going over old ground, mainly on Ortigia but also in the more modern part of Siracusa itself which we'd never really explored before.

Ortigia had changed little though there did seem to be more of a sense of urgency about bolstering up some of the older edifaces that seemed in danger of toppling into each other. Finally Ortigia was a 'work in progress'.

We lay in the sun on the rooftop terrace and read and talked to our fellow guests, always in the vain hope that

Sabrina would rush up to tell us that everything was sorted for our visit to the Teatro Greco which was, after all, why we were here. And although we loved it here and it was a place we would always return to, we both realised that we were looking forward to returning to Calabria, to sit by the pool in the shade of our ancient gnarled olive tree. Perhaps we were just getting old.

Our final day dawned and for the third morning in a row I looked enquiringly, pleadingly even, at Sabrina. And for the third time she had the same response ... she had contacted her friend and was still waiting for an answer. I reminded her that this was our last day, it was now or never.

We went out for our last walk around Ortigia and returned to Giuggiulena to make ourselves some lunch and to sit on the terrace. There was a note on the table for us from Sabrina saying that she was off to see her friend Angelina and would have some news later. Later turned out to be very much later.

In the meantime, to be or not to be, both Kay and I read once again the copy of *Ecuba* in English that I'd downloaded before we left England. We assumed that the play would be performed in classical Greek so we wanted to have some idea what was happening ... assuming we ever got there.

When we next saw Sabrina it was close to six o'clock, less than two hours till the performance. She didn't actually have any tickets for us but, nevertheless, her news deserved the massive hug we each gave her ... her friend was expecting us, all we had to do was go to the box office, ask for Angelina and all would be well.

By seven, we were at the front of the queue when the gates opened and Angelina was indeed expecting us and finally, clutching our tickets, we hired two cushions for the stone seats not realising that we had the best seats in the house

Il Teatro Greco starts to fill; half an hour later Ecuba starts her body count which already include a cushion. As it happened, two cushions proved to be much better than one.

It was a warm June evening. Seven-thirty Italian time meant nothing as gradually this ancient theatre filled. En route to our seats we walked alongside the set with its mounds of white sand, a scattering of realistic-looking bodies and the solitary tree that made it look like the desolate battlefield it was supposed to be.

Sometimes when an aspiration is finally fulfilled it can be an anti-climax. Our route to this place began some six years earlier when we first discovered Ortigia and Siracusa and first saw ourselves sitting here on some future warm summer evening; and when it eventually came to pass it was no anti-climax.

When, at ten past eight, silence finally reigned in that time-worn auditorium and a bedraggled, desperate Ecuba struggled into view and started trailing the bodies one-by-one across the sand to pile them against the tree, it was the beginnng of the most powerful and most memorable theatrical experience I have ever had.*

Quite simply it was stunning from start to finish, from the early evening sun to dusk when finally Ecuba and her fellow thesbians took their final bow to a standing ovation. Nobody, it seemed, wanted it to end; senses had been exposed and touched in a unique shared experience and, unlike more conventional theatres, nobody seemed to want to leave that place for fear of losing some of its spell.

Almost in silence we walked back down through the town and across to Ortigia in search of a quite place to eat, a place

---

For the record *Ecuba* was one of two of Euripede's plays performed on alternate evenings that year; the other, *Troiane*, was chronologically the first story. Both plays featured the character Ecuba but were performed by different casts, under different direction and with a completely different set.

where we could collect our thoughts and marvel at our good fortune to have experienced such an event in such a setting.

And we'd had a bonus ... the performance of *Ecuba* had been in Italian and not classical Greek as we'd thought so we understood more of what was happening than we expected to. Not a lot more, but enough.

We left Giuggiulena and Siracusa early the next morning for we had one final rendezvous before heading back across the Straits of Messina to Calabria ... we still had to pay our respects to Etna, finally relieved of the mist and the rain.

Since our last visit there had been a prolonged series of eruptions and we knew these had changed the mountain's profile somewhat though the route up to the summit was much as it had been before. It also seemed to cost more too; I remember the sharp intake of breath when we discovered the power of inflation and realised that we didn't have enough cash with us. We just hoped they accepted credit cards. They did.

There was a different smell too, the smell of sulphor I think, and the summit landscape had become more open, more accessible and yet more menacing. The sulphorous outcrops and the steam suggested that this place was in a state of flux, that it could and would change again soon, that, although we could hear and feel nothing, there were embryonic rumblings under foot.

Back on the *autostrada* we resisted the temptation to try once again to find somewhere to park in Taormina and headed straight for the ferry at Messina, a city transformed since our last visit only four days earlier. What a difference the sun makes.

I had been reading about Messina and was hoping to have a little time to view it with a different eye. Hitherto it was the place I had to negotiate to get from the port to the *autostrada*, a place that I escaped from in both directions. And so it would probably remain but I was now more aware of the events that I alluded to earlier, the story of the 1908 earthquake that Paulo had told me about in Reggio Calabria.

What I had never noticed before was that modern Messina has a dearth of tall buildings. This is a direct result of the earthquake in two respects; firstly many of the taller buildings were destroyed but, and this is more important, the rebuilding programme that continued well into the 1920s specifically did not include many tall buildings.

I had also come across a book by an eccentric English traveller who knew the area well and indeed was in Sicily at the time of the earthquake. At times Henry Festing Jones' *Castellinaria*, published in 1911, makes harrowing reading but, as I watched a fading Messina from the ferry taking us back to Calabria, I realised it would be difficult not to see Messina in a new light.

I also had time to glance skywards and imagine a project that had been in the news both in the UK but particularly here in and around the Straits of Messina, the building of a bridge to connect mainland Italy and Sicily.* The sea crossing is less than thirty minutes, nevertheless for some that would appear to be half-an-hour too long.

Like the Channel Tunnel project in the UK this had been a on-off idea for as long as anyone can remember – even the Romans thought about building a pontoon-like structure

---

*In March 2006 the scheme was given the go-ahead which is why it became international news; then in October the same year it was cancelled by the newly-elected Prodi government. His successor, Silvio Berlusconi, re-activated the scheme and at the time of writing it continues to be an on-going project of his government. Because Berlusconi polarises people (not unlike Margaret Thatcher), it seems that the merits (or otherwise) of the project have been lost in its association with his name.

with boats and barrels. And, like the Channel Tunnel, it is a scheme about which everyone seems to have a view.

Historically in this part of Italy monies allocated for such major works have found their way into the coffers of the *mafia* and its Calabrian incarnation, the *'ndrangheta*, and of course the area is known to have a history of earthquakes. That said, the lure of the prestige that would follow in the wake of such a scheme is attractive for many politicians, both local and national, as Italy would be home to the world's tallest and longest single-span suspension bridge.

To be or not to be ... that is the question ... I wonder if next time we're this way whether we'll be able to drive straight across?

Full circle

It was approaching seven when we arrived back at L'Oenotri where we were greeted like long-lost family; even Mara seemed pleased to see us. Salvatore came out from his kitchen to welcome us back and to tell us that he'd prepared something special.

That 'something' turned out to be a wonderful home-made ministrone soup which, Salvatore explained later, would be much better for us than a normal *antipasta* dish as we had been travelling all day. Whether or not this was true didn't really matter; what was touching was the obvious thought that had gone into his planning that day. Everybody had ministrone soup that evening, but in Salvatore's mind he had made it for us.

It didn't take long to get back into our pool-side routine and, now that we had another eleven days here, we decided to get to know the province of Crotone a little better.

We visited Crotone itself, the erstwhile home to mathematician and philosopher Pitagora or Pythagaros, he of the right-angled triangle and its hypotenuse, and didn't much take to it. On the other hand the winding cross-country route through the neighbouring towns of San Mauro and Scandale

A bird's eye view of L'Oenotri from Monte Fuscaldo

made it worthwhile and anyway San Mauro was the nearest place where we could buy petrol. Once the new road was finished, we were assured, there would be petrol once again at Siberene ... problem was that nobody knew for certain when the new, more direct road linking the town with the Cosenza-Crotone *superstrada* would be finished.

We drove to the top of the nearby Monte Fuscaldo which offered amazing views of Siberene, L'Oenotri itself, all the surrounding towns and villages and beyond to the sea at Crotone. There was a small animal sanctuary at the top and picnic tables and a pizzeria that opened on summer evenings and weekends. But the most important function of this place at this time of year was as a look-out station for fire. Calabrian summers can be blisteringly hot (being there in June we only had a taste of things to come) and there is a real risk of fire. Roberto told us that the main man up there with all this responsibility was his brother, Salvatore.

Roberto had befriended us and we also got to know two of his children, young Francesco, who had a penchant for dying the front of his hair red, and his older brother Guiseppe who also did odd jobs at the *agriturismo*, particularly with the maintenance of the pool.

One evening Roberto arranged to meet us in the square; he said he had something to show us. We were sitting at Carlo's when he appeared and followed him down out of the square and along a narrow street that wasn't made for cars but, judging by the various paint scratches on some of the walls, that didn't deter the locals.

We stopped by a rust-red metal door recessed in a stone arch while Roberto fumbled for his keys. He told us to wait while he put on some light and then called us forward into what can only be described as a cave, a stone cavern hewn out of the rock that was Siberene itself.

But this was more than a cavern it was Roberto's *cantina*, his place for making wine ... rather like Pietro's *cantina* in Sardinia only on a larger scale and without the rendered walls. Roberto beamed, he knew we were impressed, the more so when he got the glasses out and insisted that we try his wines. Not surprisingly the red wine tasted familiar for it was the same vintage as the wine we drank every evening at L'Oenotri.

On another occasion he drove us down the steep, winding track into the valley below the *agriturismo* where, surrounded by olive groves, there was an assortment of ramshackle outbuildings that were home to his pigs and in particular a huge sow and her seven offspring.

Angela, the cleaner, also became a close friend. I later found out from Elvira that we were the only clients that she ever really got to know because, by the time Angela arrived for work, any other clients were normally half-way to the coast. We broke the mould and so were invited to drop in one afternoon to meet her daughters and have a cup of coffee.

Angela's house was easy to find. It was the first house you passed when approaching Siberene from the main road, the last as you left; it had a gate with two pillars and atop each was a stone lion. Behind the gate was a wide flight of stone steps up to two small terraces behind which lived Angela with her three daughters; a fourth was married and lived in northern Italy.

We did the grand tour and could tell that Angela was proud of her home – and rightly so. She showed us photos of the children when they were young and of her late-husband, in other words we were treated like any other friend and honoured to be so.

That Sunday, because there was a lunchtime *prima cresima*,

first communion, party for about eighty guests at L'Oenotri, Salvatore asked us if we would eat at the same time, have *il pranzo* (lunch) instead of *la cena* (dinner) so that he could have a well-earned evening off. Somehow or other we became part of the extended party and ended up seated next to 'invited' guests, Angela and two of her daughters, Morena and Valeria.

This was to be our first experience of a Calabrian *festa* and the huge number of courses that this can involve. In order these can be ... *aperitivi*, *antipasti* (outside), *antipasti* (inside), *primo primo piatto*, s*econdo primo piatto*, *primo secondo piatto*, *secondo secondo piatto*, *dolci*, *frutti*, *liquori*.

No wonder Salvatore needed a rest ... and it was just as bad for us, we were totally exhausted afterwards and went to bed. It goes without saying that we didn't eat again that day.

The following Saturday, our last before we headed back up north, there was a wedding reception at L'Oenotri for nearly two hundred guests and Salvatore again asked us if we would eat at the same time and of course we agreed. This time we ate in an adjacent room and not with the other wedding guests.

Outside it was forty degrees in the shade; Roberto had been delegated to be our personal waiter. I fell asleep at the table after the fourth or fifth course and we decided to go to bed ... there were, Roberto told us, eight or nine more courses to come, not counting the massive wedding cake which we'd seen being carried in. The next morning we explained our disappearing act to a relieved Salvatore ... *he* thought there had been a problem with the food!

Footballs' World Cup was in full swing. We were keeping an eye on the progress of two teams, England and Italy. On a couple of occasions we joined the L'Oenotri 'family' in a small, otherwise private, gathering to watch the Italian games. Usually on these occasions we were joined by

Beniamina's husband Vittorio, the mild-mannered surgeon who also had a penchant for giving the television a robust piece of his mnd when things didn't quite go Italy's way. But all was well with the (Italian) world and somehow or other the team got through to the final stages of the competition. And, as everyone knows, unlike the European championships two years earlier, they did not return home empty-handed for, against all the odds, they actually won the competition.

Sadly, by this time (mid July) we were back in England and did not share this occasion with Vittorio and friends; I know it would have been a moment to cherish.

England, on the other hand, fared less well but did get through the group stages to play Ecuador.

As Carlo suggested, we went across to Pino's bar to watch the game. As Italy were not playing, Pino's was almost empty. A few local lads sat on stools, a family of four, ten-year-old son, teenage daughter, was sitting in front of the television, we sat behind them.

Our arrival seemed to revive interest in the game for the locals. The family sitting in front gave us a knowing nod of the head. We didn't really catch on at first, not until we noticed the shirt colours of the Ecuador team and the striking resemblance to the colours worn by the family sitting in front. Yes, we were are sitting in a bar, in Siberene, in Calabria, with a family from Ecuador and the local lads, privy to the irony of the occasion, were really enjoying themselves – they were probably expecting some sort of altercation.

Scoreless, the first half came and went though I noticed that the mother crossed her fingers behind her back every time David Beckham touched the ball. We all went outside at half time to stretch our legs and have a chat in the sun. The Ecuadorian family hailed from Genoa and, like us, they were on holiday; the daughter it seemed had a crush on David

Beckham so was actually a closet England supporter. Her mother explained the finger-crossing ... she said she believed Beckham to be the most dangerous player in the English team.

About fifteen minutes into the second half Beckham scored. For a few minutes there was no reaction from our Ecuadorian friends. Then, very slowly and deliberately, the mother turned round and smiled at me; I shrugged my shoulders as if to say I was not to blame. One-nil was the final score.

Nobody really cared, it was all a bit of fun; afterwards the six of us shared a drink and then, outside in the square, embraced and said our goodbyes. True to form England lost their next game to Portugal and soon joined Ecuador on their way home.

At the weekends we met another Roberto, Vincenzo's son. In his late twenties, this Roberto spoke, like Elvira, excellent English but he worked in Caserta, north of Naples which is why we saw so little of him.

Nevertheless, the few times we met were enough for Roberto to give me a nickname that, at the time, I was totally unaware of. It was over a year before someone spilt the beans, two years before anybody would tell what the name was.

Nicknames are an Italian tradition; usually they go with the name – Luigi is usually Gino, Guiseppe is Pino, Francesco is Ciccio, Antonio is Nino. Even all of these have their variants and occasionally, rather than being a diminutive, the name goes with the character ... mine was clearly the latter.

Salvatore had a nickname too and when he said we could call him Turuzzo we knew that somehow our embryonic relationship was changing.

Away from Siberene, the highlight of our Calabrian sojourn was a visit to the grammatically incorrect coastal town of

The castle at Le Castella and the castle at Siberene

Le Castella. Here there is a castle, a 16th entury Aragonese castle that sits on a pile of rocks in the sea, its only link with the mainland a narrow spit of land. It was a June day, but not a 'glorious' June day at L'Oenotri, which is why we were *in giro*, on the road in search of a fickle sun; we caught up with it at Le Castella.

The rich golden, almost orange, walls of the castle itself stood proud against the backdrop of the clouds overlooking the Ionian Sea. We walked across the spit into the castle then up to the highest point of its circular tower via a narrow stone spiral staircase from where there were spectacular views of the town itself and the coastline beyond.

We decided to return to Siberene by heading north towards Crotone and thus completing a large circular tour of the province. There was an ulterior motive in that Crotone had not impressed us first time round and Vincenzo's son Roberto suggested we take a look at another side of city, the part with beaches and bars and one particular *gelateria*.

So it was the promise of a better-than-average ice-cream that lured us back to Crotone and specifically to its more southerly waterfront. Roberto was right, this was quite a different side to the city … not a beach resort in the conventional sense, more a place for locals to pop down to during the afternoon *siesta* to lie in the sun and cool off in the water.

After a long walk along the waterfront promenade, from the edge of the town to the end of the road and back, we felt we deserved that ice-cream. And it was as good as we were led to believe.

One afternoon Beniamina asked us if we'd like to come to the opening of an exhibition at the Castle that evening and of course we accepted her invitation.

That same afternoon there arrived at L'Oenotri two large and important-looking gentlemen accompanied by their wives who occupied the two rooms next to ours. Important-looking they might have seemed but they were courteous and in no way aloof; they eyed the pool with a certain pleasure.

It was half an hour later and Kay and I were still sitting under 'our' olive tree when from behind there was a rumbling and a pounding as first one, then the other of our overweight neighbours, rushed by and hurled themselves into the pool and in so doing created their own little tsunami. Their respective wives went for the down-the-steps option.

They were having a great time and with some difficulty managed to climb the steps out of the pool only to hurl themselves back in again. Discreetly, Kay and I moved our chairs a little bit further back from the edge. We had been trying to pick up what language they were speaking and finally decided it was something East European.

It was time to dry off. Courteous to a fault they let their wives get out first; the first of the husbands exited the pool successfully but, as the second put his foot on the bottom rung of the steps, there was a loud breaking noise. The step had given way under his weight.

There followed all sorts of apologetic noises as he was finally helped out of the water followed shortly afterwards by what was left of the steps.

It was an amusing interlude, a curious spectacle, the more so for Kay and I when we went to the Castle only to discover that our two dolphins were the guests of honour, they were in fact the Russian ambassadors to Palermo and Milan and were in Siberene for the opening of an exhibition of Russian religious ikons that had been hidden away for years in the Kremlin.

We sat through an hour or so of speeches and didn't really understand very much except the bit about 'peace and friendship between our great peoples'. Religious ikons would not have been our exhibition of choice but we made the best of the occasion and in particular the opportunity it afforded to meet other people from the town and particularly Siberene's mayor (*il sindaco*), Bruno Cortese. Ironically we were also formally introduced to two slightly embarrassed Russians and their wives.

Every evening, between about six and seven-thirty we made our pilgrimage up into Siberene for our pre-prandial *aperitivo* with Carlo. And every evening at this time Siberene's *passeggiata* was in full swing.

In essence the *passeggiata* here was no different to those we had experienced elsewhere, though there was a noticeable absence of fur coats, even in the winter I would guess. Also the oval shape of the *piazza* made for a more ordered and predictable route from church to castle and back again. Every so often people sitting at the bars would get up and filter in; just as often some of those walking would slope off and bag an empty table. There were five points of entry into the square where people joined in or took off home; few, like us, headed straight across this line of traffic to get to our favourite bar.

Every evening from the safety of Carlo's bar we watched this ritual and, as is the way of routine, we couldn't help but notice the regulars and their characteristics.

The 'regulars' in rural communities such as Siberene, were mainly men; generally any women were either one half of a young couple showing their togetherness to the world or perhaps part of a small group, most often in their thirties or forties, who had probably grown up and gone to university in a world very different to that of their mothers. And of course there were the inevitable exceptions.

There was one more mature couple who were regulars but there was something else that made them different ... their little dog. It was rarely 'with' them but always knew where they were, always seemed to know which four feet, in a forest of feet, belonged to those that fed it. It would weave in and out, this way and that, it would go off to take a look at something interesting, have a sniff here or a sniff there, but it was never more than six or seven metres from those four familiar feet.

There was a young lad who always walked by himself; a man who was never without a cigarette; two teenage girls who, arm in arm, walked faster than everyone else and talked to match; one man who never seemed to be without at least one *cellulare* held against an ear; small mixed groups of young adults at the pre-couple stage, the boys trying to impress, the girls trying to look cool under pressure.

There was a group of men that argued and gesticulated a lot but seemed to be the best of friends; a man who always smoked a cigar and carried a book; a small bespeckled boy on a bicycle who went from stabilisers to independence as we watched; there were groups of older men with a life of toil written into their faces, their hands and their bodies but who always smiled and seemed to enjoy life – and were always incredibly courteous.

With the clock approaching half-seven, the *passeggiata* started to wind down. Slowly, almost inperceptibly, the square would begin to empty as, first, the 'independent' women headed home to prepare dinner, leaving the more senior (male) citizens to do a few more circuits before they too wandered off home to see what delicacy their womenfolk had prepared.

By the time the church clock struck a quarter to eight, the square would be almost empty; time for us to head back to L'Oenotri.

There was one other Siberene ritual we witnessed here in

the *piazza* on two consecutive Saturday mornings when we had stopped by at Carlo's. On the first occasion we arrived in *Piazza Campo* just as a wedding party was leaving the church. The reception was in the castle so the newly-weds walked across the square, the bride's dress trailing along the cobbles, while all around people wished them well.

As they passed Carlo's kingdom, a beaming Carlo strode forward carrying a silver platter with two glasses of bubbly, the couple stopped, raised their glasses and toasted each other while all around cameras clicked.

Toasted in style, the couple continued on their short walk to the castle, negotiating of course the usual mix of people who might be up in the square on any other Saturday morning, with or without stabilisers.

The following Saturday morning we witnessed exactly the same ritual ... different couple of course.

Carlo, it seemed, had the monopoly on this little ritual so I asked him what would happen when he got married. Clearly he had already thought this one through and quick as a flash said he'd let cousin Pino do it just this once. It was only later that I realised Pino would surely be at the wedding.

Back at the L'Oenotri *our* rituals and of those around us carried on. People came and went, the only constant, it seemed, was us and the people that worked there.

Like the sixteen bikers from Luxembourg, people often just passed through for the night; others would stay four or five nights but rarely longer than a week. One Dutch couple, trying (unsuccessfully) to evade the media's preoccupation with the World Cup, had originally planned for three nights but left after five. They were, it seemed, old hands at Italian *agriturismi* and, in embarrassingly fluent English, confided with us that here at L'Oenotri they had found "almost the most perfect".

They were not a little envious that we'd hit upon L'Oenotri first time round and suggested that if we were ever to visit any other we'd now only ever be disappointed. By chance we were able to put their theory to the test sooner than we expected.

*

And so it was that, a few days before we were due to leave Siberene, we were sitting up in the *piazza* enjoying Carlo's hospitality and partaking of a lunchtime *apertivo* when a van selling fruit and vegetables parked up across the square by the *farmacia*. The driver fancied a lunchtime tipple; he also had a penchant for catching pigeons by the feet ...

We have come full circle, but not quite to the end.

Epilogue

Our encounter with the pigeon fancier in the square not only prompted me to record some of our other experiences as we had stumbled our way through Italy but it made me realise just how much I was going to miss this place in particular.

Our original plan was to travel back to Rome via two nights at Il Pinocchio in Frascati but that afternoon I put it to Kay that if we were to stay an extra night at L'Oenotri we could try and find another overnight stop somewhere halfway, perhaps at an another *agriturismo*, before heading for Rome Campino and our late afternoon flight home.

"Do it", she said; like me she just wanted to sit by this pool with these people for one more day. Within the hour, and thanks to Elvira's computer, we had cancelled our return visit to Il Pinocchio and booked in to La Mazzarella, halfway between Siberene and the airport.

And if we hadn't stayed for that extra night we'd never have met Pupa.

Eugene Pupa was an optician in Crotone; from what Salvatore told me later, for the people of Siberene he was the *only* optician in Crotone. He and his Bulgarian girlfriend

The Sila mountains fom Siberene and lake Ampollino before the rains

were dining at L'Oenotri on our last evening. The four of us were eating outside and, as can happen on such occasions, our two tables soon became one.

Both spoke good English, much better than our Italian so, as ever, we opted for the lazy option. There was nothing particularly memorable about our conversation other than Eugene's response when I asked why he had driven thirty kilometres to eat when Crotone had dozens of restaurants. "It's simple", he said, "Salvatore is the best chef in the province."

What was memorable, however, was an evening, quieter than usual, a warm June evening under the stars with good food, good wine and good company and, for Kay and me, the last such evening for some time. All our friends at L'Oenotri whom we wouldn't see again had already said their goodbyes, as had Carlo; there would be more such emotional farewells the next morning.

Even when we said goodbye to Eugene and his girlfriend, acquaintances for no more than a few hours, it was in the certain knowledge that we'd meet again.

A night to remember for all sorts of reasons.

I won't linger on the morning of our departure, suffice to say we got on the road as soon as we could for we had one more bit of Calabria to visit en route north.

As we drove away from L'Oenotri and turned the bend for one last look up at Siberene, lit from behind by a bright, early-morning sun fending off some random clouds, we knew that no other place had touched us quite like here. We couldn't quantify it, we didn't try to; we just knew that, sooner or later, we'd be back to sit in the shade of that old olive tree.

In the meantime, we had an ancient forest to visit.

The Sila mountains dominate both sides of the *superstrada*

between Crotone and Cosenza so, having seen the view from the main road, we decided to drive through the southern range and pick up the *superstrada* closer to Cosenza.

An hour later and we had already wound our way up to and round Cotronei and into the foothills of the Sila. Always climbing and constantly marvelling at the singular beauty of our surroundings. There were few outposts of habitation, just an ever-winding road, tall trees, occasional shafts of light and an eerie silence. In the summer it is difficult to imagine that for many parts of the Sila this is the off-season, it is as winter sports centres that many of the towns make their living.

We were heading for Trepido and lake Ampollino, one of three artificial lakes in these mountains. As we climbed west, there was a noticeable drop in temperature and an increasing hint of rain in the air. Soon this became a drizzling reality though not enough to deter us from parking up to take a short walk alongside the lake. When the wind picked up and started to blow the drizzle almost horizontally it was clearly time to move on.

We skirted the eastern edge of Ampollino then cut across country via another twisting, remote road, narrower than the others, and eventually made it back to the *superstrada* to Cosenza where we picked up the *autostrada* north.

By late afternoon we had eventually found La Mazzarella, an *agriturismo* in the foothills of Mount Tubenna east of Salerno (see map on page 174), an *agriturismo* quite unlike L'Oenotri.

The main difference was in the agricultural and produce side of the business; at L'Oenotri it was always in the background, here at La Mazzarella it was more part of the whole experience.

The 'calm and serene environment' that the website promised was no exaggeration and we enjoyed an hour-long tour of the 'estate' with the owner before sitting out on the verandah of our room in anticipation of dinner. Unlike at L'Oenotri we had little choice but to eat in – the thought of negotiating the lanes back to civilization was not appealing. Not that there was anything wrong with our evening meal, it was excellent home-cooked fare, though not the five courses that Salvatore prepared every evening.

I'm almost ashamed to say it but we missed the pool and, although we would have been happy to spend a few days here, unlike L'Oenotri it was not the sort of *agriturismo* where we could easily have whiled away two or three weeks. And this I think is the essence of the different types of *agriturismo* that our Dutch friends had talked about.

Apart from the obvious differences in to what extent an *agriturismo* is or is not a working farm or a place that produces just enough for its own needs, there is the question of accessibility, the immediate and greater environment and the on-site facilities. Taking all these aspects into consideration it is easy to see why it was the Dutch couple decided to extend their stay at L'Oenotri – after all, for them, it was "almost the most perfect" *agriturismo* they had found.

Likewise our night at La Mazzarella had enabled *us* to stay one more night at L'Oenotri and for that we were grateful. Shortly after breakfast next morning we were back on the *autostrada*; Rome Ciampino beckoned.

We had almost a year to reflect on the best of times.

*

For the next two summers we returned to Siberene and L'Oenotri and took up residence in 'our' room and under 'our' olive tree, by 'our' pool, for two weeks the first year and three weeks the second.

The first year we travelled south and returned the slow way, via Rome Ciampino and six nights at other places in-

The late Roberto Sculco at home in his *cantina*

between, three en route to Calabria, three on the way back. These overnight stops included two other *agritursmi*, only one of which, Agriturismo Carretiello near Roccadaspide in the Cilento (see map on page 174), was even close to L'Oenotri.

The following year we decided to cut out the middle man by flying with Alitalia from London to Rome and from Rome on to Lamezia Terme; we left London in the morning and by late afternoon we were in Siberene rekindling friendships.

At L'Oenotri our routines changed little. We spent much of the time relaxing by the pool and chatting to friends. Of course we made the odd foray into the surrounding towns and countryside but on the whole we were happy to be in and around Siberene.

From the second year there was a new face at L'Oenotri, a young Romanian lad, Guilliano, who turned his hand to almost everything, from waiting to pool maintenance. Like everyone else there he soon became a good friend.

The third year there was one face fewer; our friend Roberto died in February that year. He was a much-loved, larger-than-life, generous man and the first person we met in Calabria.

The previous year we had sensed that Roberto wasn't one hundred percent but it hadn't stopped him trying to shock us by showing off the small abbatoir where he dispatched the animals for L'Oenotri's table. I still recall the wicked grin on his face when he opened a large fridge to reveal the partially dressed skull of a cow. He was trying to shock and was duly impressed by our reaction, or lack of it.

Our circle of friends grew both at L'Oenotri and in the town's *piazza* where people recognised us from previous years and increasingly made conversation.

We got to know Salvatore's wife and children and ate with them one evening. We renewed our acquaintance with

Vincenzo's son Roberto, now Crotone-based, and found that we had a lot more in common that our age-difference would suggest. We also met Roberto's brother, Sergio, and their mother Silvana and Beniamina's daughter Alma and her husband. We stopped off once at Trebisacce, Elvira's home town, and had a pre-lunch *aperitivo* with her amazing grandmother.

The waiter Martino succumbed to our charms and that straight back of his relaxed and we gained another friend who called us *fratello-sorrella* because he said we were like brother and sister. Martino also made everyone laugh when he fantasized about dancing with Kay under a star-lit sky (while I slept). It never happened.

And of course we dropped in at Angela's more than a few times for a coffee and a chat.

We sat at Carlo's and watched the *passeggiata* and observed how people changed year on year ... we even found out that the little dog was called *Briciola*, which means breadcrumbs. Here it was that Carlo first introduced us to his *fidanzata*, his fiancée Anna-Marie; they planned to marry in September 2009.

We renewed our friendship with Pupa and dined together one evening at a wonderful fish restaurant in Crotone and he ate with us several times at L'Oenotri.

The new road changed from being a work-in-progress the second year to becoming a reality the third and made life much easier. The long-awaited petrol station, on the other hand, remained in the 'still pending' tray.

Towards the end of our third and longest stay at L'Oenotri, we decided it was time for a change. We had already hinted to Elvira that we would be back the following year so we thought it best if we speak to her first … and asked if we could see room 5 as we'd heard other guests wax lyrical about the so-called 'honeymoon suite'.

We booked it.

*

It was eight o'clock on a hot July morning in 2008, our last at L'Oenotri for another year. We had said all our goodbyes, save two, Vincenzo and Guilliano. We had to be on our way to Lamezia by eight-thirty.

Uncharacteristically Guilliano, on breakfast duty that morning, didn't turn up and wasn't answering his mobile. Vincenzo was worried but knew he had to focus on preparing breakfast for us and the half a dozen other guests itching to get off to the sea. We thought we would make life easier for him and forego breakfast that morning, we could always pick up something at the airport. Vincenzo was insistent that we should eat before we left.

Still no Guilliano and it was time to go. Our farewell to Vincenzo was a hasty affair as he struggled with the coffee machine. Our drive to Lamezia was peppered with speculation about what might have happened to Guilliano.

*

In early August Roberto told me the whole story in an email; in the same email he confirmed that he had found us a house.

In mid-September, ten weeks after we left Calabria, we packed our new(-ish) left-hand-drive car and drove to Folkstone, the first leg of our journey back to Siberene to live. Naturally we spent our first night there in room 5 at L'Oenotri.

Why and how is, as they say, another story …

Selected Bibliography

Castellinaria and other Siciian Diversions by Henry Festing Jones (AC Fifield 1911)

The Mother by Grazia Deledda, translated by Mary G Steegmann; Introduction by DH Lawrence (Jonathan Cape 1928)

South to Sardinia by Alan Ross (Hamish Hamilton, 1960)

Sea and Sardinia by DH Lawrence (William Heineman 1964)

Midnight in Sicily by Peter Robb (Harvill Press 1998)

The Dark Heart of Italy by Tobias Jones (Faber and Faber 2003)

Cosa Nostra by John Dickie (Hodder and Stoughton 2004)

The Force of Destiny: A History of Italy since 1796 by Christopher Duggan (Penguin / Allen Lane 2007)

Niall Allsop ...

... was born and educated in Belfast, Northern Ireland, but began his working life as a primary school teacher in London and in 1971 took up his first headship.

He left teaching in 1981 to pursue a career as a freelance photo-journalist specialising in the UK's inland waterways and wrote extensively in this field both as a contributor to several national magazines and later as author of a number of related titles, one of which, in a fourth edition, remains in print.

By the early '90s he was a graphic designer and the in-house designer for a photographic publishing house in Manchester before becoming a freelance graphic designer based in the south-west of England.

In September 2008 – the point at which this book ends – he and his wife, Kay, moved to Calabria, the toe of Italy, where they enjoy a sort of retirement and where they continue to struggle daily with the language in a small hilltop town where they are the only English-speaking people.

As you might expect the move itself and its aftermath are the subject of a third title, *It's never what you expect: making the move to Calabria*.

Niall Allsop is also the author of *Keeping up with the Lawrences: Sicily, Sea and Sardinia revisited* – see overleaf.

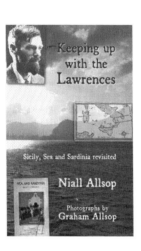

Keeping up
with the
Lawrences

Sicily, Sea and Sardinia revisited

Niall Allsop

Photographs by
Graham Allsop

Keeping up with the Lawrences

Sicily, Sea and Sardinia revisited

In January 1921 DH Lawrence and his wife, Frieda, left their Taormina home in north-east Sicily and set off on a nine-day excursion to and through Sardinia and back to Sicily via mainland Italy. Lawrence's account of their journey, *Sea and Sardinia*, was published later that year in New York.

Keeping up with the Lawrences is a contemporary account of making the same journey, as far as possible keeping to the same route, the same timescale, the same mode of transport and the same overnight stops as Lawrence and the queen-bee, his pet name for Frieda.

Like *Sea and Sardinia*, *Keeping up with the Lawrences* is written in the present tense but there the comparisons end for the irascible Lawrence was not a tolerant traveller, was not what the Italians would call *simpatico*. Only rarely did he initiate a conversation; only twice did someone buy him a drink!

Lawrence travelled at a time of heightened tensions in Europe after the Great War and these are reflected in his outlook and the people he encountered, most of whom he gave appropriate nicknames such as Hamlet, the Bounder, Mr Rochester and the Sludge Queen.

Niall Allsop and his nephew traversed the same route in a different world, a brave new world of iPods and tele-communications masts, and here they met Julius Caesar and Cicero, Wonderwoman, Red and Mr Irritable ... and many more colourful and interesting characters brought to life on the pages of this unique travelogue.

Also includes over forty black & white images and four maps, including the original drawn by Lawrence himself.

11192186R0